Canadian Wild Game Cookbook

*Jeff Morrison
and James Darcy*

www.companyscoming.com
visit our website

Dedication

This book honours the memory of Alfred Morrison, Ronald Swail and other close hunting companions I have lost over the years. You will forever be in my heart and travel with me each fall to the majestic Laurentian Mountains. May your presence remain at hunt camp for an eternity.

Canadian Wild Game Cookbook

Copyright © Company's Coming Publishing Limited

First Printing August 2014

Library and Archives Canada Cataloguing in Publication
Morrison, Jeff, 1967-, author
        The Canadian wild game cookbook / Jeff Morrison, James Darcy.
(Wild Canada series)
Includes index.
ISBN 978-1-927126-69-1 (pbk.)
        1. Cooking (Game). 2. Cooking, Canadian. 3. Cookbooks.
I. Darcy, James, author II. Title. III. Series: Wild Canada series
TX751.M67 2014   641.6'91   C2014-900819-8

Published by
Company's Coming Publishing Limited
87 East Pender Street
Vancouver, British Columbia, Canada V6A 1S9
Tel: 604-687-5555 Fax: 604-687-5575
www.companyscoming.com

We gratefully acknowledge the following supplier for their generous support of our Test and Photography Kitchens: Campers' Village (p. 88).

Company's Coming is a registered trademark owned by Company's Coming Publishing Limited.

We acknowledge the financial support of the Government of Canada through the Canada Book Fund for our publishing activities.

Printed in China

PC: 27

Table of Contents

Big Game
Deer
Elk
Moose
Caribou
Pronghorn
Bison
Wild Boar
Bear

Small Game
Rabbit
Muskrat
Beaver

Game Birds
Goose
Duck
Grouse
Pheasant
Quail
Woodcock
Wild Turkey

Other Wild Game
Frog

Introduction

As a country, Canada has traditionally focused on its renewable natural resources more than just about any other country in the world. Being as resource-based as we are, with a long and celebrated history of hunting and gathering, it should come as no surprise that wild game is as important to the Canadian diet as it is.

Long before European settlers arrived, aboriginal communities incorporated game meat in their diet, the animals taken through various methods of harvest including hunting and trapping. The reliance upon renewable natural bounty remains an important aspect of aborginal life today.

Wild game and conservation are extremely important aspects of the Canadian economy within native and non-native communities alike. From what I have seen over the years, however, the use and management of natural resources in this country is somewhat controversial. Some schools of thought maintain that preservation of nature is the way to go, and that no wild game resource should be harvested or tampered with in any way. The more conservation-minded people understand that selective and controlled management and harvest of our fish and game are required to maintain game populations at sustainable levels.

The merits and health benefits of wild game meat have never been disputed. Regardless of whether you choose elk, caribou, deer, moose or any other large game species, or one of the many fabulous small game animals such as hare, grouse, goose or wild turkey, wild game meat is the purest and healthiest food you could possibly serve. Game meat is typically low in fat and cholesterol, high in protein and is not loaded with growth hormones or any unwanted chemicals. Wild game is all-natural and pristine—like the water in a cold mountain stream—with a unique flavour and texture.

In this cookbook I hope to share some insight into the vast assortment of game species our country has to offer, from the field to the table. In my 30-plus years as a passionate and responsible hunter and conservationist, I have learned first-hand the benefits of game meat. For those who enjoy tasty, natural, well-thought-out meals straight from the mountains and meadows of our great land, this cookbook will come in handy. By sampling just a small handful of recipes within these pages, you may soon understand why wild game truly is nature's most perfect food.

Working with Wild Game

Cooking wild game may seem difficult or intimidating to those with little experience, but trust me, you do not need to be an avid hunter or conservationist to become a successful wild game chef. You just need to be slightly adventurous. By following a few basic concepts and reading through the recipes in this book, you will find that cooking game meat can be the most natural thing in the world because, after all, it is so naturally Canadian.

Most wild game meats you will find in stores are commercially prepared for cooking. They will typically be pre-packaged and frozen, while some cuts may require a bit of extra trimming or fine-tuning on your part. Wild meat butchers and specialty shops take extra care when preparing game meats for the table so that you do not have to. Any special techniques you may require to prepare a certain dish will be described in *Tips* scattered throughout this book.

Preparing and Field-dressing Wild Game

If you plan to hunt for your own wild game, there are a few things you should know. The field-dressing and early meat preparation stage is the most important step when it comes to the quality of game meats. Anyone who works directly on wild game following its harvest needs to wear rubber gloves. Some important things to remember while field-dressing your game, without getting too graphic, are such things as being careful not to cut into organs or allowing fluids to drain onto the meat. Bacteria will set in as soon as the animal has expired, so it is imperative that you cool and dry your meat as soon as possible. Freshly harvested game meats should be cleaned and washed with cool water. It is also your responsibility to have your meat hung for the aging process as soon as possible. Well-treated wild game always produces the best final product when it hits the table.

Caring for Game Meat at Home

As with conventional meats, wild game meat requires great care when freezing, preparing and storing. Specialty butchers will most often vacuum-pack the various cuts of meat immediately following the butchering and cutting process. This type of packing has the effect of locking in the flavour. Meats packaged in air-tight vacuum-packs, with thick, freezer-grade plastics, are the best for long-term storing. Meat sealed in this manner will stay fresh for one year or more in the freezer without risk of freezer burn or frost damage.

Wildlife Conservation

The ethical side to cooking with wild game meats can be a controversial subject. Whether you are an avid hunter or not, it should be noted that any and all game meats featured in this book can and should be harvested in both a legal and ethical manner. Hunting rules and regulations are established by each province, not only to limit the number of animals taken but also to help manage and maintain healthy wild game populations. Hunting and habitat management are key components to conservation and serve to ensure the sustainability of our renewable natural resources.

A Few Helpful Tips

Wild Game Breakfast Quiche

Serves 6

Who says real men don't eat quiche? Served as an alternative to the traditional bacon and eggs in the morning, this wild game breakfast quiche may just be the tastiest early morning meal you've had yet. As an avid hunter and breakfast creater for six hungry sportsmen at camp each year, I think that this wild game breakfast quiche will be the answer to my prayers. I can easily prepare it the night before, which will be a real time-saver in the morning. With the alarm bell usually ringing around 3:30 AM, an extra half hour sleep will certainly be appreciated.

> 1/2 lb (225 g) bacon, diced
> 1 medium onion, diced
> 1/2 lb (225 g) ground venison sausage (smoked)
> 1 x 2 lb (900 g) bag frozen diced hash browns
> 12 eggs
> 1/2 lb (225 g) shredded Cheddar cheese

Place bacon, onion and sausage in Dutch oven and cook over medium until meat is browned. Add hash browns. Meanwhile, in separate bowl, beat eggs together. Once the hash brown mixture has cooked for 15 minutes and the potatoes have begun to brown, pour the beaten eggs over top and cook until eggs have started to set, 10 to 15 minutes. Add cheese over eggs and cook for 10 more minutes, until eggs set completely and cheese melts. Slice and serve.

Venison Breakfast Sausage Patties

Makes about 5 dozen sausages

This venison recipe is what I would call somewhat of an anomaly. Ninety percent of the venison sausage recipes you will find are for dinner sausages, and usually involve a smoker and making a pepperoni- or pepperette-type sausage. A good breakfast sausage recipe using venison is difficult to find. The great thing about making up a large batch of sausage is that you can freeze it in sizeable packages for later use. This venison sausage is moist, tender and every bit as good as pork or beef sausage.

(continued on next page)

6 lbs (2.7 kg) ground venison
2 lbs (900 g) ground pork
1/4 cup (60 mL) curing salt
1 Tbsp (15 mL) pepper
1 Tbsp (15 mL) dried crushed chilies
1/4 cup (60 mL) brown sugar
3 Tbsp (45 mL) dried sage

2 Tbsp (30 mL) butter

Place venison and pork in very large bowl. Add remaining ingredients. Mix well to incorporate. Fry small piece in frying pan to ensure that seasoning is to your taste.

Divide into eight 1 lb (454 g) portions and freeze. When ready to use, thaw one portion and form into 6 to 8 patties. Melt butter in skillet over medium and cook sausage patties, turning occasionally, until browned and cooked through.

Pictured on page 33.

Try with This

Hash Brown Casserole

Serves 12

1 x 2 lb (900 g) bag frozen hash brown potatoes
1/2 cup (125 mL) butter, melted
1 x 10 oz (284 mL) can condensed cream of chicken soup
1 cup (250 mL) sour cream
1/2 cup (125 mL) diced onion
2 cups (500 mL) shredded Cheddar cheese
1/2 tsp (2 mL) salt
1/2 tsp (2 mL) pepper
1/4 cup (60 mL) butter
2 cups (500 mL) crushed cornflakes cereal

Preheat oven to 350°F (175°C). In large bowl, combine hash browns, first amount of butter, soup, sour cream, onion, cheese, salt and pepper. Mix well and transfer to large casserole dish.

In small pot over medium, melt second amount of butter and sauté cornflakes until lightly browned. Pour over hash browns. Bake, uncovered, for about 40 minutes, until golden brown on top.

Roast Leg of Venison

Serves 8

Who says venison isn't tender and moist? Once you have mastered the roast leg of venison, you will never hear complaints of tough, dry meat again. The trick to this recipe is knowing when your roast has thawed out completely, without leaving it so long that the natural juices begin to leach out. A properly thawed leg of venison will be soft and pliable without any internal juices having yet escaped. The next important thing is not to overcook the roast. Oven time depends greatly on the thickness of the roast, so check it often. The great thing about a roast leg of venison is the leftovers. When using leftovers for sandwiches, slice it thin and add a little pepper and salt. I prefer using buttered bread and mayo, while other guys in camp enjoy it with mustard.

1 x 2 to 3 lb (900 g to 1.4 kg) venison roast

3 cups (750 mL) water
1 cup (250 mL) clam tomato beverage
1 cup (250 mL) sliced celery
1/2 cup (125 mL) red wine vinegar
1/4 cup (60 mL) sugar
2 garlic cloves, minced
1/2 tsp (2 mL) salt
1/2 tsp (2 mL) pepper

Make sure roast is thawed. Pat dry and set aside.

In large mixing bowl, combine remaining increadients. Place roast in bowl; roll to make sure it is well coated in mixture. Cover bowl and refrigerate overnight to marinate. Roast may even be marinated for 1 full day if you like.

Preheat oven to 350°F (175°C). Remove roast from marinade and pat dry, then place in roasting pan. Cook, uncovered, for 1 1/2 hours, checking for doneness after 1 hour. Meat should be slightly pink in middle; do not overcook. Let stand for 5 minutes before serving.

Deer

Venison Tenderloin with Pear Chutney

Serves 4 to 6

Not only is venison low in fat, high in protein and completely healthy for you, it has to be the most versatile protein of any I have ever known. After serving white-tail dinners in a variety of traditional ways, I began experimenting with some new and, what I would describe as new-age techniques and ways of serving venison. Venison Tenderloin with Pear Chutney is one of those recipes I have fallen in love with.

2 pears, peeled, cored and chopped
1/4 cup (60 mL) sugar
2 Tbsp (30 mL) apple cider vinegar
1 small chili pepper, diced
1 garlic clove, minced
1 small piece ginger root, minced
1 cinnamon stick
1 pinch ground cloves

1 tsp (5 mL) dried thyme
1/2 tsp (2 mL) salt
1/2 tsp (2 mL) pepper
2 lbs (900 g) venison tenderloin

For chutney, place first 8 ingredients in small frying pan. Stir and cook over low until sugar has dissolved. Raise heat to medium and simmer for about 15 minutes, until pears are soft. Remove and discard cinnamon stick.

Preheat oven to 350°F (175°C). In small bowl, mix thyme, salt and pepper. Place meat in roasting pan. Rub thyme mixture into meat. Cook for about 20 minutes, until desired doneness is reached. Let stand for 5 minutes before serving with chutney.

Pictured on page 34.

Roast Rib of Venison

Serves 8

This recipe just cries out to be served in an outdoor setting, but I haven't figured out why. The scent of the roast as it nears completion brings me back to a simpler time when our forefathers lived off the fat of the land, hunting and gathering and enjoying the fruits of their labour. There is something about the aroma of wild game that makes me think of my heritage and my hunting roots. Whatever the case, roasted venison is the perfect meal to be served at the cottage or while camping, hunting or on any other outdoor adventure.

3 Tbsp (45 mL) lemon juice
3 Tbsp (45 mL) water
1 x 4 to 5 lb (1.8 to 2.2 kg) venison rib roast

1 Tbsp (15 mL) dry mustard
1/2 tsp (2 mL) salt
1/2 tsp (2 mL) pepper
1/2 tsp (2 mL) garlic powder
1/4 cup (60 mL) steak sauce
bacon drippings

Combine lemon juice and water in large bowl, and place meat in it, turning to coat, allowing liquid to soak in.

Preheat oven to 325°F (160°C). In small bowl, combine dry mustard, salt, pepper and garlic powder. Mix and add steak sauce to form paste. Rub paste onto meat. Stand roast in shallow pan and spread top generously with bacon drippings. Cook for about 1 hour, until just slightly pink inside. Let stand for 5 minutes before serving.

Canadian Roast Venison

Serves 8

One of the great things about Canadian Roast Venison, besides the name, is the ability to mix and match several different cuts of meat. Provided you follow the instructions carefully in the roasting process, your finished product should be mouth-watering. It's a recipe we often use at hunt camp during the autumn deer season because it's a favourite of the men, and there are always enough leftovers for sandwiches to bring out in the bush the next day.

(continued on next page)

Deer

1 x 4 to 5 lb (1.8 to 2.2 kg) venison roast
1 Tbsp (15 mL) Dijon mustard (with whole seeds)
1 tsp (5 mL) pepper
1 tsp (5 mL) garlic salt
1 x 355 mL can Canadian lager (or pilsner)

Preheat oven to 350°F (175°C). Place roast in roasting pan and rub with mustard. Sprinkle pepper and garlic salt over roast. Cook, uncovered, for about 30 minutes. Remove pan from oven, add beer and cover pan. Lower heat to 275°F (140°C), and return pan to oven. Cook for about 3 hours, basting every 20 minutes or so, until centre is slightly pink. Do not overcook. Let stand for 5 minutes before serving.

Barbecued Venison Ribs

Serves 4

Not only is white-tailed deer hunting an ecologically sound and healthy activity, but it is also a tradition passed down through the generations. In my family, my great-grandfather passed on his love and appreciation of the great outdoors to my grandfather, who passed it on to my father and down to me. The great Canadian hunt camp has become somewhat of a legend for its long-standing heritage among many families in this country. I would not be the person I am today if I had not been taught to appreciate the great outdoors and the knowledge of game conservation and hunting.

2 cups (500 mL) clam tomato beverage
1 cup (250 mL) water
1 x 3 to 4 lb (1.4 to 1.8 kg) rack venison ribs

1/2 cup (125 mL) barbecue sauce

Preheat oven to 250°F (120°C). Place juice and water in bottom of large roasting pan. Place ribs on rack inside roasting pan (so they are not sitting in juices) and cover. Cook for 3 hours. Remove ribs from oven and allow to cool.

Preheat grill to medium. Brush ribs with barbecue sauce and place on grill. Cook for 5 minutes per side. Remove from grill and serve.

Easy Venison Chops

Serves 4

Most deer meat taken by hunters is that of the male, or buck. As part of sound wildlife management, a certain number of antlerless deer must be harvested each year to achieve a fine population balance. The meat of a young deer or fawn is comparable to veal in beef, and the meat of the doe, or female deer, is similar to the buck—although, depending on age, it has a tendency to be more tender than that of the male. Either way you look at it, venison is delicious and unique.

2 garlic cloves, minced
1/4 cup (60 mL) red wine vinegar
1/4 cup (60 mL) ketchup
1 Tbsp (15 mL) vegetable oil
1 Tbsp (15 mL) Worcestershire sauce
1 tsp (5 mL) dry mustard
1 tsp (5 mL) salt
1/8 tsp (0.5 mL) pepper
4 venison chops or steaks

In bowl, combine first 8 ingredients and mix well. Place chops in large resealable plastic bag, pour in marinade and seal bag (or place in large bowl and cover). Refrigerate for minimum 2 hours.

Preheat broiler. Remove chops from bag and place in shallow baking dish (discard marinade). Place chops under broiler about 3 inches (7.5 cm) from heat and cook for about 8 minutes per side, until meat has reached desired doneness. Let stand for 5 minutes before serving.

 Try with This

New Potatoes

Serves 4

1 lb (454 g) small potatoes, such as fingerling, washed
1 Tbsp (15 mL) extra-virgin olive oil
1 tsp (5 mL) dried crushed rosemary
1/4 tsp (1 mL) salt
1/4 tsp (1 mL) pepper

In large pot, boil potatoes in water for about 15 minutes, until just cooked through. Drain. Add olive oil and rosemary, and fry over medium-high until potatoes begin to brown. Season with salt and pepper.

Deer

First Ginger Venison

Serves 4

This recipe reminds me of my first deer-hunting trip, more than 30 years ago. I was a young 13-year-old boy in a camp of men, and it was a weekend of firsts for me. Within one day, I had experienced my first wild venison meal using ginger, cooked in camp by my Uncle Alfie, and the following day was my first experience hunting, during which I was fortunate to harvest my very first deer on the first day of the season. I don't believe it all sank in that year, but it sure was an exciting time for one young country boy.

> 3 Tbsp (45 mL) vegetable oil
> 1 onion, thinly sliced
> 1 garlic clove, minced
> 2 tsp (10 mL) minced ginger root
> 1 lb (454 g) venison steak, thinly sliced
>
> 1 cup (250 mL) water
> 1/4 cup (60 mL) soy sauce
> 2 Tbsp (30 mL) brown sugar
> salt and pepper
>
> 1 Tbsp (15 mL) cornstarch

In large skillet over medium, heat oil and sauté onion, garlic and ginger for 3 to 5 minutes, until onion is soft. Add venison and cook until browned.

In small bowl, combine water, soy sauce, brown sugar, and salt and pepper to taste. Mix well; pour over meat in skillet and continue to simmer for about 10 minutes, until meat is tender.

Add cornstarch slowly to thicken sauce (you can use more or less than 1 Tbsp (15 mL) depending on how it thickens). Let stand for 5 minutes before serving.

Old Veni Stew

Serves 4 to 6

Perhaps the single greatest wild game dish for non–wild game enthusiasts is an old-fashioned venison stew. Although deer meet is one of the best red meat proteins out there, it does have a characteristically bold and somewhat gamey flavour that some people have not acquired the taste for. Time to serve up a big batch of Old Veni Stew, I say! For whatever reason—perhaps it's the seasoning or the simmering time—deer meat prepared with this recipe has virtually no gamey flavour. It is a hearty and tasty dish that will appeal to any stew lover.

2 lbs (900 g) venison stewing meat
1/2 tsp (2 mL) salt
1/2 tsp (2 mL) pepper
1/4 cup (60 mL) flour

3 Tbsp (45 mL) butter
2 onions, chopped
1 tsp (5 mL) brown sugar
1/2 tsp (2 mL) garlic powder

4 tomatoes, diced
1 cup (250 mL) sliced mushrooms

Season venison with salt and pepper. Dredge meat in flour.

Heat skillet over medium, and add butter, onion, brown sugar and garlic powder. Cook for 5 minutes, until onions soften. Add meat and cook for 5 minutes.

Put meat mixture into stew pot. Place tomatoes and mushrooms over top, and simmer for 15 minutes, until slightly reduced.

Pictured on page 69.

Venison Chili

Serves 6

Who doesn't enjoy a big bowl of chili? It just happens to be my daughter's favourite meal, and Venison Chili is every bit as good as traditional chili con carne and is another popular way of using deer meat, which becomes virtually undetectable as wild game for anyone who eats it. The venison in this recipe adds a distinct flavour to the chili, yet not so overbearing that it will turn people off. It is a fabulous recipe that can be served to guests at the cottage, and it also makes a great meal for a Sunday night at hunt camp.

1/4 cup (60 mL) butter
1 onion, diced
3 garlic cloves, minced
1/4 cup (60 mL) brown sugar
3 cups (750 mL) dry red wine
1/4 cup (60 mL) red wine vinegar
1/4 cup (60 mL) tomato paste
4 cups (1 L) chicken broth
1 tsp (5 mL) ground cumin
1/2 tsp (2 mL) cayenne pepper
1/2 tsp (2 mL) chili powder
1/2 tsp (2 mL) salt
1/2 tsp (2 mL) pepper

10 slices bacon, diced
2 lbs (900 g) venison stew meat, trimmed and finely diced
1 x 19 oz (540 mL) can black beans, rinsed and drained

In large pot over medium, melt butter and sauté onion and garlic for 3 to 4 minutes. Add brown sugar and cook for 3 minutes. Add red wine, vinegar, tomato paste, chicken broth, cumin, cayenne pepper, chili powder, salt and pepper, and stir well. Simmer for about 30 minutes, until mixture is reduced by about half.

In separate frying pan over medium-high, fry bacon for about 4 minutes, until browned. Push bacon to one side of pan and add venison on other side. Sauté venison for about 15 minutes, until well cooked. Mix in black beans. Add meat mixture to pot with wine mixture. Stir well. Simmer for 20 minutes. Serve with fresh bread or dinner buns.

Mexican-style Venison Stew

Serves 6 to 8

When it comes to stew, or even deer meat for that matter, one can never have too many recipes from which to choose. This venison stew adds a spicy Mexican twist to the usual middle-of-the-road dish. As with other stew recipes, it tends to get better with age, and often the leftover stew is better than the first time around. It will keep for approximately five days in the refrigerator, provided it is stored in a sealed container.

3 lbs (1.4 kg) venison, cut into 1-inch (2.5 cm) cubes
3 medium onions, diced
3 large carrots, diced
6 medium potatoes, cubed
2 green peppers, diced

1 x 28 oz (796 mL) can diced tomatoes
2 x 14 oz (398 mL) cans red kidney beans
1/4 cup (60 mL) flour
3 Tbsp (45 mL) sugar
1 Tbsp (15 mL) minced garlic
1 Tbsp (15 mL) chili powder
2 tsp (10 mL) jalapeno pepper sauce
3/4 tsp (4 mL) salt
3/4 tsp (4 mL) pepper

In large pot, cook venison until browned. Add onions, carrots, potatoes and green pepper, and continue cooking for 5 minutes.

Add remaining ingredients. Stir and cook for 1 hour, until vegetables are tender and meat is cooked, stirring often to avoid sticking to the bottom of pot.

Pictured on page 70.

Slow Cooker Venison Strogano.

Serves 4 to 6

Any meal prepared in a slow cooker, in my opinion, has got to be the most time-efficient meal you can choose, and this venison stroganoff is no exception. Once you have the ingredients cut up and prepared, you do nothing more than throw them in the slow cooker and let a slow simmering heat take over, turning your venison into a delectable dish for your family or friends. This particular recipe also has the effect of creating a mild flavour with very little toughness to the meat, while producing a marriage of rich flavouring, accented by the venison, in the dish as a whole.

> 1 Tbsp (15 mL) canola oil
> 1 1/2 lbs (680 g) venison stew meat, cut into 1-inch (2.5 cm) cubes
> 1 small onion, thinly sliced
> 1 x 10 oz (284 mL) can sliced mushrooms, drained
> 3 cups (750 mL) prepared beef broth
> 3/4 tsp (4 mL) pepper
> 1/2 tsp (2 mL) salt
>
> 8 oz (225 g) whole-wheat penne pasta
> 1 cup (250 mL) sour cream

In large frying pan over medium-high, heat oil and fry venison until well browned on all sides. Remove meat from pan and place in slow cooker. Add onion, mushrooms, beef broth, pepper and salt. Cook on Low for 8 to 10 hours.

About 30 minutes before you are ready to eat, add pasta to slow cooker and cook until noodles are tender. Stir in sour cream and serve.

Dutch Oven Venison with Sour Cream

Serves 4 to 6

I am an animal lover at heart. Throughout the year, I feed deer in my backyard. The property adjacent to our home does not allow hunting, and I would be disappointed if they did, as the deer we see regularly have become like friends. But how can you befriend the white-tailed deer on one hand, and pursue them in fall with a rifle on the other? Well, as an active conservationist, I understand that hunting and harvesting a certain number of animals is part of wildlife management, and that hunters do not harvest deer because they dislike them, but the contrary; most hunters I know are animal lovers like myself.

2 lbs (900 g) venison, cut into 1-inch (2.5 cm) cubes
3/4 tsp (4 mL) salt
3/4 tsp (4 mL) pepper
3 carrots, sliced
4 celery ribs, sliced
3 cups (750 mL) dry white wine

2 Tbsp (30 mL) butter
2 Tbsp (30 mL) flour
1/2 cup (125 mL) hot water
2 cups (500 mL) sour cream

Preheat oven to 350°F (175°C). Season venison with salt and pepper, and place in Dutch oven with carrots and celery. Add wine. Cover and cook for 2 hours.

Melt butter in large skillet. Add flour and mix until a paste forms. Add hot water, mix and then add sour cream. Stir until smooth. Remove venison and vegetables from Dutch oven and place in skillet. Cover and simmer for 1 hour, adding water if sauce becomes too thick. Serve with fresh bread.

Deer

Venison Pie

Serves 4 to 6

Few people realize that the white-tailed deer is one of the most closely managed of all game animals in North America. Provincial Natural Resource Departments spend a lot of money monitoring the population, establishing the appropriate hunting seasons and managing habitat. The white-tailed deer is an adaptable animal, a hearty animal, yet it is also very fragile and vulnerable to disease and depredation and is particularly susceptible to harsh weather conditions during winter.

> 2 lbs (900 g) venison round (inside) steak
> 1/2 cup (125 mL) flour
> 1/4 cup (60 mL) extra-virgin olive oil
> 1 cup (250 mL) dry red wine
> 1/2 tsp (2 mL) salt
> 1/2 tsp (2 mL) pepper
>
> pastry for 2 crust 9-inch (23 cm) pie

Slice venison into small chunks, then dredge pieces, one by one, in flour. Heat olive oil in large skillet over medium and brown meat. Add wine, salt and pepper. Lower heat and simmer for 30 minutes.

Preheat oven to 400°F (205°C). Line pie dish with pastry. Transfer meat mixture to pie dish and cover with pastry. Bake for about 20 minutes, until crust is golden brown.

Try with This

Steamed Butternut Squash

Serves 4

1 butternut squash
1/3 cup (75 mL) butter
1 Tbsp (15 mL) brown sugar

Cut squash into 4 to 6 pieces and remove seeds. Place in vegetable steamer in pot with water in bottom. Cover and steam for about 30 minutes, until squash can be easily pierced with fork. Let cool. Spoon out squash into cooking pot, discarding skin. Mash squash. Add butter and brown sugar and reheat.

Traditional Venison Tourtière

Serves 8

The combination of ground pork and venison is traditional one in the Québec tourtière or meat pie. The ground pork adds moisture and a bit of fat, while the ground venison provides the beautiful wild flavouring to this dish. You will see several regional variations of tourtière in francophone Canada. Many areas of New Brunswick and Québec offer the same basic pie, yet adding various twists in seasoning and introducing new flavours. Tourtière is a wonderful meal for a large family or group and is best served with thick brown gravy.

1 lb (454 g) ground venison
1 lb (454 g) lean ground pork
1 1/2 cups (375 mL) chopped mushrooms
3/4 cup (175 mL) diced celery
3/4 cup (175 mL) prepared chicken broth
1 cup (250 mL) cooked and mashed potato
2 onions, diced
4 garlic cloves, minced
1/2 tsp (2 mL) salt
1/2 tsp (2 mL) pepper
1/2 tsp (2 mL) dry mustard
1/2 tsp (2 mL) ground sage
1/4 tsp (1 mL) ground cinnamon

2 x pastry for 2 crust 9-inch (23 cm) pie
1 egg yolk, beaten

Preheat oven to 400°F (205°C). In large bowl, mix together first 13 ingredients. Set aside.

Line 2 pie dishes with pastry. Carefully spoon in filling, cover each pie with top crust, then seal and trim edges. Brush egg yolk over both crusts and cut holes to vent steam. Cover each pie with foil and bake for 30 minutes. Remove foil and bake for an additional 30 minutes, until crusts are golden brown.

Deer

Venison Shepherd's Pie

Serves 4

Part of the excitement for a deer hunter is the possibility of one day harvesting a true trophy animal. For me, that day came on November 4, 1996, in the mountains behind our camp. The magnificent 8.5-year-old buck I took that day remains a provincial record for Québec in the typical category, and it is a specimen the calibre of which I will never see again. What is most surprising about "Old Toothless," as this buck has become known, was how it somehow managed to make it through seven hunting seasons on open land. Evidently he was one wily old devil.

1 Tbsp (15 mL) extra-virgin olive oil
1 onion, chopped
1 garlic clove, minced
1/4 cup (60 mL) chopped carrot
1 lb (454 g) ground/minced venison
1/2 tsp (2 mL) salt
1/2 tsp (2 mL) pepper

1 x 10 oz (284 mL) can cream-style corn
4 medium potatoes, boiled and mashed
3 Tbsp (45 mL) butter

Preheat oven to 400°F (205°C). Heat oil in cast-iron skillet over medium high. Add onion, garlic and carrot, and cook for 5 minutes, until onions have softened. Add venison, season with salt and pepper, and cook until meat is browned.

Transfer meat mixture to baking dish. Cover with creamed corn, and then top with mashed potatoes. Spread out evenly with a knife and dollop butter on top. Bake for 30 minutes, until top browns.

Tasty Venison Meatballs

Makes about 4 dozen meatballs

I don't know about you, but there is nothing I enjoy more than a big plate of hearty meatballs. Meatballs made with premium white-tailed deer meat are just one of the many ways to serve nature's most conservation-minded food. If you enjoy beef meatballs, you will be ecstatic over venison meatballs. This recipe is another easy one to prepare, and everyone will enjoy the final product.

2 lbs (900 g) ground venison
1/2 cup (125 mL) bread crumbs
2 eggs, beaten
1 onion, finely chopped
2 garlic cloves, minced
1 cup (250 mL) shredded Italian cheese blend
1/2 tsp (2 mL) dried crushed chilies
2 Tbsp (30 mL) barbecue sauce

2 cups (500 mL) barbecue sauce
1/2 tsp (2 mL) pepper

Preheat oven to 375°F (190°C). In large bowl, combine venison, bread crumbs, eggs, onion, garlic, cheese, dried crushed chilies and first amount of barbecue sauce. Mix all ingredients together. Form into 1-inch (2.5 cm) meatballs, and place on rimmed baking sheet. Cook meatballs for 45 minutes to 1 hour, until well browned.

In medium bowl, combine second amount of barbecue sauce and pepper. Transfer to chafing dish and add meatballs. Serve as an appetizer or as a meal with a side dish.

Pictured on page 142.

Grilled Venison Burgers

Serves 8 to 10

It has often been felt that wild game meats such as deer, elk, caribou and moose are not suitable for grilling. I remember years ago, at my camp, the first time I discovered that wild game meat is very difficult to cook over the grill. The final product was dry and rather tough and tasteless—until I discovered this venison burger recipe. Try it, and you will not be disappointed.

> 2 lbs (900 g) ground venison
> 1/2 tsp (2 mL) *each* salt and pepper
>
> 8 to 10 hamburger buns
> 1 head romaine lettuce, washed and torn
> 1 red onion, thinly sliced
> 2 red tomatoes, thinly sliced
> 2 avocados, peeled and sliced
> assorted sliced cheeses
> 1 lb (454 g) bacon, fried crisp

Fashion 8 to 10 equal-sized patties out of your venison and place them on a baking sheet. Season with salt and pepper. Preheat grill to medium and place patties on grill. Cook until desired doneness, about 4 to 5 minutes per side for medium-rare, longer for well done.

Put your cooked patties inside hamburger buns and serve with desired fixings.

Pictured on page 160.

Try with This  **Beefeater-style French Fries**
Serves 2

6 cups (1.5 L) vegetable oil
2/3 cup (150 mL) sugar
2 cups (500 mL) warm water
2 large potatoes skin on, sliced into 1/2-inch (12 mm) strips
salt

Preheat oil in deep-fryer to 375°F (190°C). In medium bowl, dissolve sugar in water. Add potatoes and soak for approximately 15 minutes. Remove potatoes and dry thoroughly on paper towels. Deep-fry potatoes until golden. Drain on paper towels and season with salt to taste.

Venison Sloppy Joes

Serves 4 to 6

I don't care who you are, Sloppy Joes make one fine meal, but with venison meat, the Sloppy Joe takes on a whole new meaning and taste. Many people find the distinct flavour of deer meat to add a certain *Je ne sais quoi* to a Sloppy Joe. This recipe makes a great lunch or dinner and can be served all year long. If you're tired of having burgers all the time, this recipe is the one for you. My kids love it.

> 2 lbs (900 g) ground venison
> 1 medium onion, chopped
> 1 1/2 cups (375 mL) chili sauce
> 1 cup (250 mL) ketchup
> 1/2 cup (125 mL) water
> 2 Tbsp (30 mL) Worcestershire sauce
> 1 Tbsp (15 mL) prepared horseradish
> 1 tsp (5 mL) dried crushed chilies
> 1 tsp (5 mL) garlic powder
> 1 tsp (5 mL) salt
> 1 tsp (5 mL) pepper
> 1/2 tsp (2 mL) celery seed
>
> 4 to 6 hamburger buns

In large frying pan, cook venison until no longer pink. Add remaining ingredients and mix well. Simmer for 20 minutes.

Serve on hamburger buns.

Deer

Curried Leftover Venison

Serves 4

An interesting aspect of white-tailed deer behaviour and biology is their fall rutting or mating. White-tailed deer display a distinct hierarchy when it comes to breeding during the rut. The more dominant bucks will be the first to mate with receptive does, followed by males lower in the ranks. When an old dominant buck has become too frail, he will quickly be replaced by a more fit younger animal. As harsh as this may sound, it is nature's way of maintaining the most positive genes and carrying the best lineage through the various year classes. It is nature's way of ensuring survival of the fittest.

1/4 cup (60 mL) vegetable oil
1 cup (250 mL) chopped onion
3 celery ribs, chopped
2 apples, minced
2 tsp (10 mL) curry powder
2 cups (500 mL) prepared beef broth
1 1/2 tsp (7 mL) Worcestershire sauce
1/4 tsp (1 mL) hot pepper sauce
1/4 tsp (1 mL) ground ginger
1 tsp (5 mL) salt
1/8 tsp (0.5 mL) pepper

1 Tbsp (15 mL) water
2 Tbsp (30 mL) flour

2 lbs (900 g) cooked venison, cubed
1 cup (250 mL) evaporated milk
1 egg yolk, well beaten

Heat oil in skillet and sauté onion, celery and apple until golden brown. Add curry powder and simmer for 5 minutes. Add broth, Worcestershire sauce, hot pepper sauce, ginger, salt and pepper, and simmer for an additional 20 minutes.

In small bowl, mix water with flour to make a paste. Add paste to apple mixture and cook for 5 minutes, stirring constantly until thickened. Remove from heat and allow to stand for 1 hour.

Reheat sauce and add meat, evaporated milk and egg yolk. Heat, stirring, just to a simmering point, but do not boil. Serve over rice.

Deer Jerky

Makes about 2/3 lb (300 g) jerky

Deer jerky, for those who enjoy salt meat or jerky meat, is another great way to use that venison in your freezer. I love making up a big batch of deer jerky and having enough for the entire year. Jerky will last a very long time, and it makes a fabulous snack while out camping, hunting or fishing. In fact, I keep a few strips of deer jerky in my fanny pack during the hunting season. This protein-rich food is simple to store and will come in handy on the occasions when there is no time for preparing a large meal. And any nutritionist will tell you that a protein-rich snack will provide more usable energy than a sugary snack.

> 3 Tbsp (45 mL) vegetable oil
> 2 lbs (900 g) venison, cut into 1/4-inch (6 mm) strips
> 1 tsp (5 mL) salt
> 1 tsp (5 mL) pepper
>
> 2 Tbsp (30 mL) Worcestershire sauce
> 2 Tbsp (30 mL) soy sauce
> 2 garlic cloves, minced
> 3 Tbsp (45 mL) brown sugar
> 2 tsp (10 mL) cayenne pepper
> 2 Tbsp (30 mL) molasses
> 1 cup (250 mL) water

Heat oil in skillet. Add venison and season with salt and pepper. Cook until browned. Set aside to cool.

Combine remaining ingredients in large bowl. Add venison. Cover and refrigerate overnight.

Preheat oven to 175°F (80°C). Remove venison strips from marinade with tongs and shake off excess liquid. Lay venison strips out on large baking sheet and place in oven for 2 1/2 hours. Turn strips over and place back in oven for 30 minutes with door propped open 2 to 3 inches (5 to 7.5 cm).

Note: The low temperature and door propped open allows the meat to dry out and cure completely.

Elk Tenderloin

Serves 4

The elk is a majestic big game animal native to western Canada. It has experienced substantial growth in its population over the past 20 years. Folks who live in mountain towns like Banff and Jasper have become well acquainted with members of the elk family. These animals now can be seen regularly on golf courses, in parks and occasionally strolling down the street. The elk falls in size between the white-tailed deer and the moose, and it is characterized by the male's famous bugling call. Each fall, the bull elk gathers a harem of females, and his distinctive bugle can be heard rolling through the mountains as he beckons his ladies.

> 2 Tbsp (30 mL) butter
> 1 Tbsp (15 mL) chopped shallots
> 2 cups (500 mL) prepared beef broth
> 1/4 cup (60 mL) dry red wine
> 1/4 cup (60 mL) Port wine
> 1/4 cup (60 mL) hip jelly
>
> 1 1/2 lbs (680 g) elk tenderloin
> salt and pepper

In a small pot, melt butter and sauté shallots until they start to brown. Add broth and both wines, and simmer until liquid is reduced by about two-thirds. Strain mixture using fine-mesh sieve. Add jelly, return to heat and cook until sauce thickens. Set side.

Preheat oven to 425°F (220°C). Season tenderloin with salt and pepper (or any seasoning you prefer). Heat frying pan and sear tenderloin on all sides. Place in roasting pan and cook for approximately 15 minutes for medium doneness (adjust cooking time to your preferred doneness). Let stand for 5 minutes before serving. Slice, and drizzle warm sauce over meat.

Pictured on page 51.

Slow Cooker Elk Roast

Serves 4 to 6

Perhaps the most distinctive thing about elk, besides their regal appearance and bugling call, is the size and shape of their antlers. A mature bull is often categorized as a 4 x 4, a 5 x 5 or a 6 x 6, referring, to the number of points on each side of his impressive crown. As with other members of the deer family, antler size is a reflection of age, quality of habitat and genetics. Antler size also serves as a status symbol among the herd. The older, more dominant bulls possess a large, sweeping set of antlers with 10 to 12 points. Basically, the larger the elk's rack, the more likelihood of gathering a strong harem for breeding.

1 x 2 to 4 lb (900 g to 1.8 kg) elk roast
salt and pepper
1 large onion, cut in quarters
2 cups (500 mL) prepared beef or vegetable broth
1/8 tsp (0.5 mL) ground thyme
1/8 tsp (0.5 mL) ground savory

4 large potatoes, cut in quarters
6 large carrots, chopped
1 to 2 Tbsp (15 to 30 mL) flour

Place elk roast in slow cooker, and sprinkle with salt and pepper to taste. Add onion, broth and herbs and cover slow cooker. Cook on High for 3 to 4 hours.

Add potatoes and carrots, and continue to cook for another 2 hours, until meat and vegetables are tender. Add flour and stir until sauce is thickened. Serve with fresh bread.

Stuffed Wapiti

Serves 4

Why do male elk gather large harems of females during the breeding season? Well, elk and most members of the deer family are polygamists. The male is expected to take several mates each fall. The harem concept includes the gathering of cow elk in a confined area until such time that they become receptive for breeding and go into estrus. The dominant bulls in the herd increase their chances of spreading their progeny by assembling together the greatest number of females they can for the longest period.

> 2 lbs (900 g) elk flank
>
> 2 Tbsp (30 mL) butter
> 1/2 cup (125 mL) sliced fresh mushrooms
>
> 3 Tbsp (45 mL) black olive tapenade
> 6 anchovy fillets
> 2 Tbsp (30 mL) butter

Slice elk flank down centre, about 2/3 through. Open it and flatten to 1 1/2 inches (4 cm) thick, like an open book.

Melt first amount of butter in skillet over medium and cook mushrooms for 5 to 7 minutes, until tender.

Preheat oven to 400°F (205°C). Spread tapenade on meat and arrange mushrooms and anchovy fillets on top. Fold meat back over and tie with kitchen string. Rub flank with second amount of butter and place in roasting pan. Cook for about 40 minutes, until slightly pink in centre. Let stand for 5 minutes before serving.

Elk

BBQ Elk Ribs

Serves 6

With a solid well-established population of elk in central Ontario, the very first hunting season was launched in that province in 2011. The Ministry allowed the harvesting of a select number of animals without jeopardizing this burgeoning herd. Hunters and conservationists in the province are part of the reason that elk have fared so well. Conservation groups and donations by hunters and the Ontario Federation of Anglers and Hunters have contributed huge amounts of money to managing this population and establishing a huntable herd. The Ontario elk hunt has continued, with a controlled number of animals taken each year. Even with annual hunting, the population of elk in the province continues to rise.

> **3 lbs (1.4 kg) elk ribs, cut in pieces**
>
> **1 onion, diced**
> **1 cup (250 mL) ketchup**
> **2 Tbsp (30 mL) white vinegar**
> **2 Tbsp (30 mL) lemon juice**
> **2 Tbsp (30 mL) brown sugar**
> **1 Tbsp (15 mL) prepared mustard**
> **1 tsp (5 mL) salt**
> **1/4 tsp (1 mL) pepper**

Preheat oven to 300°F (150°C). Brown ribs in cast-iron pan for 3 minutes per side and set aside.

In bowl, mix together next 8 ingredients to make sauce. Place ribs in casserole dish and cover thoroughly with sauce. Cook for 3 hours, frequently basting ribs with sauce.

Venison Breakfast
Sausage Patties (p. 8)

Venison Tenderloin with Pear Chutney(p. 11)

Baked Elk Steaks

Serves 6

When cooking with wild game, you can mix, match and interchange different red meat species in the recipes. Although this particular recipe calls for elk steaks, you may quite easily substitute deer steak or perhaps moose, provided you adhere to special directions in the thickness or size and cut of each meat. Most red wild game meats are quite similar, so although each has its own unique properties, you can try a different species next time around.

>1 cup (250 mL) bread crumbs
>1/2 cup (125 mL) flour
>1/2 tsp (2 mL) salt
>1/2 tsp (2 mL) pepper
>6 elk steaks, 1 inch (2.5 cm) thick
>1 egg, beaten
>
>1/4 cup (60 mL) canola oil
>1 onion, chopped
>1 cup (250 mL) sliced mushrooms
>1/2 cup (125 mL) water

Preheat oven to 300°F (150°C). Mix bread crumbs, flour, salt and pepper in shallow dish. Dip steaks in egg, then in crumb mixture.

Place oil in cast-iron skillet over high. Sear steaks for 2 minutes per side, then transfer to roasting pan. Cover steaks with onion, mushrooms and water. Cook, covered, for 1 1/2 hours.

Try with This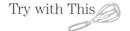

Canadian Baked Potatoes

Serves 2

2 large Russet potatoes
canola oil, enough to coat potatoes
salt, sprinkle

Preheat oven to 350°F (175°C). Wash potatoes and pierce with fork several times (to allow steam to escape). Coat potatoes with canola oil and sprinkle with salt. Place potatoes on baking sheet and bake for about 1 hour, turning halfway through.

Elk Cabbage Rolls

Serves 6

As the elk population in western Canada expanded, so too did hunting opportunities for this great beast. As a result, the number of great elk recipes has also exploded in recent years. I would say the elk is quite similar in taste and texture to the moose. Like other Canadian wild game, the elk is an extremely lean meat, so it requires great care in cooking and preparation. You will notice throughout this book that many of the recipes stress the cooking times and temperatures.

12 large cabbage leaves

1 tsp (5 mL) beef bouillon powder
1 lb (454 g) ground elk
1 lb (454 g) sweet Italian sausage
1/2 x 6 oz (170 g) can tomato paste
1/2 cup (125 mL) warm cooked rice
1 Tbsp (15 mL) butter
1 egg
1 tsp (5 mL) salt
1/4 tsp (1 mL) pepper
1/2 tsp (2 mL) dried basil
1 tsp (5 mL) garlic powder
1 tsp (5 mL) onion powder
1 Tbsp (15 mL) paprika
2 Tbsp (30 mL) diced onion
2 Tbsp (30 mL) diced celery
1/4 cup (60 mL) shredded carrot

2 cups (500 mL) tomatoes, crushed
1/2 x 6 oz (170 g) can tomato paste
1 cup (250 mL) water
1 tsp (5 mL) beef bouillon powder
1 1/2 Tbsp (22 mL) brown sugar

Boil cabbage leaves for 3 minutes, until they are limp. Remove and set aside.

(continued on next page)

36   Elk

Transfer 1/2 cup (125 mL) of hot water that cabbage leaves sat in to large bowl, and stir in first amount of bouillon powder until dissolved. Add elk, sausage, first amount of tomato paste, rice, butter, egg, salt, pepper, basil, garlic powder, onion powder, paprika, onion, celery and carrot. Mix.

Preheat oven to 325°F (160°C). Lay out cabbage leaves. Divide meat mixture evenly onto cabbage leaves. Tuck sides and roll to cover meat, and place in lightly greased roasting pan.

Combine remaining 5 ingredients together in pan; heat and stir until sugar and bouillon powder are dissolved. Pour over cabbage rolls. Place roasting pan in oven and cook for 1 hour and 45 minutes.

Curried Elk

Serves 6

Elk, also known by the name wapiti, are closely related to the European red deer. In Canada, elk have traditionally been a western game species; however, thanks to management efforts in Manitoba and Ontario, the majestic elk is becoming established in those provinces in several small pockets of localized populations. In 2011, for the first time in nearly 100 years, the province of Ontario opened a short, controlled elk-hunting season in the central area of the province. It is the feeling of biologists and hunters in Ontario that the elk hunt will be around for many years.

> 2 Tbsp (30 mL) extra-virgin olive oil
> 1 garlic clove, minced
> 1 onion, chopped
> 2 lbs (900 g) elk meat (chuck or brisket),
>   cut into 1-inch (2.5 cm) cubes
> 1 cup (250 mL) water
> 1 Tbsp (15 mL) beef bouillon powder
> 2 tsp (10 mL) curry powder
> 1 x 7 1/2 oz (213 mL) can tomato sauce

Heat cast-iron skillet over high and add olive oil, garlic and onion. Cook for 5 minutes, until onions have softened. Add elk meat and brown on all sides. Add water, bouillon powder, curry powder and tomato sauce. Cover and simmer for about 1 hour, until liquid is slightly reduced.

Elk Chili

Serves 8

Cooking elk can be tricky but is not impossible. As with other wild game meats, elk tends to dry out; never add salt during the cooking process because it will draw out the moisture and create a dry, tough final product. Another tip used by many chefs is to cover the meat and let it rest for at least 5 minutes after it has cooked to allow the moisture to be better retained. Never cook elk at temperatures higher than medium-high. If you prefer your meat well done, opt for a recipe that uses a marinade.

2 Tbsp (30 mL) vegetable oil
2 cups (500 mL) diced onion
1 cup (250 mL) diced celery
1 red pepper, diced
2 garlic cloves, minced
2 lbs (900 g) ground elk

2 Tbsp (30 mL) chili powder
1 1/2 tsp (7 mL) dried oregano
1 tsp (5 mL) ground coriander
1/2 tsp (2 mL) cayenne pepper
2 x 28 oz (796 mL) cans diced tomatoes
2 x 14 oz (398 mL) cans tomato sauce
2 x 5 1/2 oz (156 mL) cans tomato paste

2 x 14 oz (398 mL) cans red kidney beans, drained and rinsed
salt, optional

Heat oil in large pot over medium-high. Add onion, pepper, celery and garlic and cook for 5 to 7 minutes, until softened. Add elk to pot and fry for about 10 minutes, until no longer pink.

Add chili powder, oregano, coriander and cayenne pepper and stir. Add tomatoes, tomato sauce and tomato paste. Bring mixture to boil and then reduce heat. Simmer for 30 minutes, stirring occasionally.

About 15 minutes before serving, stir in kidney beans and heat for 15 minutes. Season to taste with salt.

Elk Enchiladas

Serves 4

The majestic elk is distinctive for its large crown of antlers. Because the antlers are shed each year, they provide a renewable natural resource that is very popular in the art world. During late fall and early winter, when elk have finished the mating ritual and the rut is over, the large antlers are shed one at a time so that they may free up their energy to battle the cold winter ahead. The antlers can be found scattered on the ground in elk country and, if discovered before small mammals use them as food, they can be used to create decorative pieces such as rustic chandeliers, knife handles and other accessories.

> 1 lb (454 g) ground elk
> 1 medium onion, chopped
> salt and pepper
>
> 1 x 14 oz can (398 mL) chilli, no beans
> 2 x 14 oz cans (398 mL) tomato sauce
>
> 8 x 8-inch (20 cm) round tortillas
> 2 cups (500 mL) grated Cheddar cheese

In skillet over medium-high, brown ground elk and onion. Season with salt and pepper to taste. Once meat has fully cooked, drain and set aside.

In small pot, combine chilli and tomato sauce and heat on low.

Warm tortillas in baking dish in low-temperature oven for 1 or 2 minutes. Remove tortillas and turn oven up to 350°F (175°C). Put 1/8 of meat in centre of 1 tortilla and top with 2 tbsp (30 mL) cheese. Roll up and place seam-side down in baking dish. Repeat for remaining tortillas, meat and cheese. Pour chili mixture over filled tortillas and top with remaining 1 cup (250 mL) cheese. Bake for about 30 minutes, until bubbling occurs.

Great Elk Casserole

Serves 6

Since you can never have too many wild game casseroles, I suggest you try this one using the delicious meat of the elk. As convenient as the Great Elk Casserole is, it is the fact that it appeals to so many people that makes it such a great meal; not only for a camp full of hungry hunters, but also for your family at home. This casserole is very mild without the typical gamey taste, meaning both you and the kids will enjoy it. It took some convincing to get my sometimes finicky girls interested, but eventually they caught on.

> 2 Tbsp (30 mL) canola oil
> 1 lb (454 g) elk meat, cut into 1-inch (2.5 cm) cubes
> pepper
> 4 Tbsp (60 mL) flour, divided
>
> 2 large onions, thinly sliced
> 2 garlic cloves, minced
>
> 2 cups (500 mL) beer
> 2 cups (500 mL) prepared beef broth

In large steep-sided cast-iron skillet, heat oil on medium-high. Season elk meat with pepper, then roll in 1 Tbsp (15 mL) flour, then drop in hot oil. Brown meat, then transfer to large casserole.

Add onions and garlic to same skillet, lower heat and cook for 10 minutes, until softened.

Preheat oven to 325°F (160°C). Add remaining flour and beer to skillet, increase heat and bring to a boil. Simmer for 10 minutes, until slightly reduced. Pour over meat in casserole, then add broth. Cover and cook in oven for 1 hour. Remove from oven and let stand for 5 minutes before serving.

Quick Moose Roast

Serves 6 to 8

It is always interesting to me when I hear people who either don't agree with hunting or just aren't all that adventurous, food-wise, speak of wild game and how they refuse to even try it. My in-laws were against wild game until I served them perhaps the best meal they had ever eaten. It was a moose rib roast, and, being cooked to perfection, beautiful, natural aromas were wafting from the kitchen. My father-in-law commented at how great it smelled, and I replied, "You haven't seen anything yet." It didn't take more than a couple of bites for them to be convinced that wild game meat, and in particular the moose they were enjoying that evening, was better than most over-the-counter cuts.

> 1 x 3 lb (1.4 kg) moose roast
> 1 Tbsp (15 mL) dry mustard
> 2 x 1 1/4 oz (38 g) envelopes onion soup mix
> 1 tsp (5 mL) salt
> 1 tsp (5 mL) pepper
> 6 medium potatoes, halved
> 2 carrots, chopped
> 2 celery ribs, chopped
> 2 cups (500 mL) chopped tomatoes

Preheat oven to 350°F (175°C). Rub roast thoroughly with dry mustard and sprinkle it with onion soup mix. Season with salt and pepper. Place roast in roasting pan and surround with potatoes, carrots and celery. Pour tomatoes over top. Cover and cook for 2 hours. The roast is done when slightly pink in centre. Let stand for 5 minutes before serving.

Try with This  ## Baked Asparagus

Serves 4

1 lb (454 g) fresh asparagus
1 Tbsp (15 mL) extra-virgin olive oil
1 tsp (5 mL) salt
1 Tbsp (15 mL) balsamic vinegar

Preheat oven to 400°F (205°C). Break tough end off of each spear of asparagus using your hands (the best way to cut asparagus). Place spears in shallow roasting pan and drizzle with olive oil and sprinkle with salt. Roll asparagus around so that they are evenly coated. Cook for approximately 15 minutes, until they have reached desired tenderness. Remove from oven, drizzle with balsamic vinegar and serve.

Smoked Moose Tenderloin

Serves 4

Without exaggeration, moose tenderloin is about as perfect a red meat as one could ever ask for. When processed and aged properly, the tenderloin, or blackstrap as it is often called, will be melt-in-your-mouth tender and loaded with natural flavour. What this largest member of the deer family is famous for—unlike the more common white-tailed deer—is the extremely mild, non-gamey flavour. Most inexperienced game eaters would never be able to tell that it is, in fact, wild game. So dig in and enjoy a little slice of perfection from the north woods on your dinner table.

> 1 garlic clove, minced
> 2 Tbsp (30 mL) teriyaki sauce
> 2 tsp (10 mL) white vinegar
> 2 Tbsp (30 mL) brown sugar
> 1/4 tsp ground ginger
> 1 Tbsp (15 mL) whole cloves
> 2 lbs (900 g) moose tenderloin

In saucepan, combine first 6 ingredients and heat until sugar is dissolved. Cool somewhat. Transfer marinade to large resealable plastic bag, and add tenderloin. Seal bag and turn until meat is coated. Refrigerate overnight.

Remove meat from marinade and place on smoker grill. Pour remaining marinade into smoker's water pan along with 3 quarts (3 L) of water. Add 2 wood sticks and smoke for 3 hours. Let stand for 5 minutes before serving.

 tip MAKE MARINADE BEFORE LEAVING

If you are planning to cook this recipe at the hunt camp or cottage, prepare the marinade before you go, and remember to transport it in a good quality sealed container.

Moose Kebabs

Serves 3 to 4

The moose (*Alces alces*) is the largest member of the deer family. An adult moose can weigh up to 540 kilograms. There are four subspecies of moose in North America. From largest to smallest they are the Alaska moose (*A. a. gigas*), found in Alaska and the western Yukon; the western moose (*A. a. andersoni*), found from British Columbia and the Yukon to western Ontario; the eastern moose (*A. a. americana*), found in eastern Ontario, Québec and the Atlantic provinces; and a small localized population of Shiras moose (*A. a. shirasi*) found throughout the Rocky Mountains of Canada and the United States.

1/4 cup (60 mL) teriyaki sauce
1 Tbsp (15 mL) peanut butter
1 tsp (5 mL) brown sugar
1 tsp (5 mL) garlic powder
1/2 tsp (2 mL) hot sauce
1 lb (454 g) boneless moose meat,
   cut into 1-inch (2.5 cm) cubes

1 onion, cut into 1-inch (2.5 cm) pieces
1 green pepper, cut into 1-inch (2.5 cm) pieces
2 cups (500 mL) small mushrooms

In medium bowl, combine teriyaki sauce, peanut butter, brown sugar, garlic powder and hot sauce. Mix well, then add moose cubes and stir to coat. Cover and refrigerate for 1 hour.

Preheat grill to medium. Remove moose meat from marinade (reserving marinade for basting later) and thread onto skewers, alternating with onion, pepper pieces and mushrooms. Grill for 10 to 15 minutes turning occasionally and basting with reserved marinade, until meat is cooked.

Moose Steak with Mushroom Gravy

Serves 2

To produce a good-quality moose steak, certain procedures need to be followed. A quick and humane harvest, aging and good butchering are all essential components of producing quality moose meat. On one trip into northeastern Quebec many years ago, we were served moose tenderloin, harvested that morning. The remainder of the tenderloin was placed in the camp fridge. Almost a week later, we had another meal of that same moose meat. Just from those few days of aging in the fridge, the meat had become much more tender.

2 moose steaks (cut of your choice)
3 Tbsp (45 mL) bacon drippings
1/2 cup (125 mL) prepared beef broth
1 medium onion, chopped
1/2 tsp (2 mL) garlic powder
3 Tbsp (45 mL) tomato paste
1/2 cup (125 mL) water

1 cup (250 mL) sliced mushrooms
2 Tbsp (30 mL) flour
1/4 cup (60 mL) cream
salt and pepper

In a large skillet, fry steaks in bacon drippings for 5 to 7 minutes, until brown on both sides. Add broth, onion and garlic powder to skillet. Dilute tomato paste in water and add to skillet. Cover and simmer for about 1 hour, until meat is tender.

Remove steaks from skillet and cover to keep warm. Add mushrooms to skillet. Cover and simmer for 5 minutes. Remove cover and add flour. Stir. Add cream. Stir. Add salt and pepper to taste. Serve mushroom gravy over hot steak.

Summer Moose Brochettes

Serves 4

I will never forget my up close and personal encounter with a moose family group. It was the year 2000, and my brother-in-law, Steven Enright, and I were trout fishing in northwestern Québec when we heard a commotion at the far end of the lake. As we approached the bay, we could see that two young calf moose were stranded in the lake with Mom waiting for them on the shoreline. These calves were only a few days old, judging by their shaky legs and uncoordinated bodies. Mom moose watched as we did our best to direct the two calves toward a section on the shoreline where they could climb ashore. It wasn't long before they were reunited with Mom, as if nothing had happened.

    1/4 cup (60 mL) vegetable oil
    1/4 cup (60 mL) wine vinegar
    1/4 cup (60 mL) ketchup
    1 garlic clove, minced
    1 Tbsp (15 mL) Worcestershire sauce
    1 tsp (5 mL) salt
    1 tsp (5 mL) pepper
    1/2 tsp (2 mL) dry mustard
    1 lb (454 g) moose steak, cut into 1-inch (2.5 cm) cubes

    1 red pepper, cut into chunks
    1 yellow pepper, cut into chunks
    1 cup (250 mL) mushrooms, stems removed
    1 cup (250 mL) cherry tomatoes

Mix first 8 ingredients together in large bowl. Place meat in bowl and stir to coat. Cover and refrigerate for 12 hours.

Preheat grill to medium. Remove meat from bowl and pat dry. Alternately thread meat and vegetables onto metal (or wooden; remember to soak in water for 30 minutes ahead of time) skewers. Brush with extra marinade and grill for 15 minutes, turning often. Serve with white or wild rice on side.

Pictured on page 52.

Slow Cooker Moose Spaghetti Sauce

Serves 6

Of all the moose recipes in this book, this one has to be the most convenient and my personal favourite. For me, this spaghetti sauce is a great addition to the fishing season and the hunting season. Each spring, my father and brothers-in-law and I bring one meal of this moose spaghetti sauce on our fishing trip into northwestern Québec. Besides all the fantastic fresh trout, it's probably the meal that we look forward to the most.

2 Tbsp (30 mL) vegetable oil
1 onion, diced
1 red pepper, diced
3 garlic cloves, minced
1 bunch fresh parsley, finely chopped
1 lb (454 g) ground moose
1/2 cup (125 mL) dry white wine

1 x 28 oz (796 mL) can diced tomatoes
2 Tbsp (30 mL) tomato paste
1/2 tsp (2 mL) cayenne pepper
1/2 tsp (2 mL) salt
1/2 tsp (2 mL) pepper
1 cup (250 mL) water

Heat oil in large pot over medium, and cook onion, red pepper, garlic and parsley for 5 to 7 minutes, until soft. Add meat and cook for another 5 minutes, until it is no longer pink. Add wine and cook for about 10 minutes, until it is nearly evaporated.

Transfer meat mixture to slow cooker. Add remaining ingredients and simmer on Low for 8 hours. Serve over spaghetti.

European Moose Ragu

Serves 4

The moose is a family oriented species. An adult cow usually has her first calf in her second or third year, and she always has a single newborn. A cow moose of four to five years old will have twins and occasionally triplets, and very rarely, quadruplets. As with other members of the deer family, the female calves remain with the mother throughout much of their early life, at least the first two to three years, and they form what is known as a family group—typically consisting of an older cow moose, two females from a previous year and one or possibly two calves from the current year. The males leave the family group after the first year.

>   2 Tbsp (30 mL) extra-virgin olive oil
>   1 medium onion, chopped
>   2 garlic cloves, minced
>   1 lb (454 g) moose steak, finely chopped
>   1 x 14 oz (398 mL) can plum tomatoes, drained
>   2 tsp (10 mL) tomato paste
>   1 cup (250 mL) dry red wine
>   1/2 tsp (2 mL) salt
>   1/2 tsp (2 mL) pepper

Heat oil in large skillet over medium-high, and then add onion and garlic. Cook for 5 minutes, until softened. Add meat and cook until browned. Add plum tomatoes, tomato paste, wine, salt and pepper. Mix well. Cover and simmer for 15 minutes. Serve over your choice of pasta.

Try with This  **Classic Caesar Dressing**

Serves 6

3 garlic cloves, minced
1/4 cup (60 mL) olive oil
3 Tbsp (45 mL) mayonnaise
3 Tbsp (45 mL) grated Parmesan cheese
1 Tbsp (15 mL) white wine vinegar
2 tsp (10 mL) Dijon mustard
1/2 tsp (2 mL) salt
1/2 tsp (2 mL) pepper

Whisk together all 8 ingredients in bowl until smooth. Store in any leftover dressing in refrigerator.

Moose Shepherd's Pie

Serves 4

The most exciting part about moose hunting is using a call to entice a bull moose toward you. The moose is a highly vocal animal, especially during the fall rut, which begins around mid-September in central Canada. The cow in estrus will emit a long, bellowy, plaintive call to announce to all local bull moose that she is receptive and ready for breeding. It is this call that hunters often imitate during the hunting season.

2 Tbsp (30 mL) vegetable oil
1 lb (454 g) ground moose
1 medium onion, diced
1 x 10 oz (284 mL) can condensed cream of chicken soup
1 x 14 oz (398 mL) can cream-style corn
6 medium potatoes, boiled and mashed

Preheat oven to 350°F (175°C). Heat oil in medium skillet over medium-high. Add meat and onion; cook until meat has browned. Spread cream of chicken soup into bottom of large casserole dish. Layer meat mixture over top of soup, then pour corn over meat and spread out evenly. Then spread mashed potatoes over top. Cook for 40 minutes, until top has browned slightly.

Try with This  **Mixed Bean Side Salad**

Serves 6

1 x 14 oz (398 mL) can cut green beans, drained
1 x 14 oz (398 mL) can cut wax (yellow) beans, drained

2 Tbsp (30 mL) chopped fresh oregano
2 Tbsp (30 mL) extra-virgin olive oil
2 Tbsp (30 mL) red wine vinegar
1 garlic clove, minced
1/2 tsp (2 mL) salt
1/2 tsp (2 mL) pepper
1/2 onion, thinly sliced

Transfer beans to bowl of ice water.

In large bowl, whisk together oregano, olive oil, vinegar, garlic, salt and pepper. Add onion. Drain beans and add to onion mixture. Toss to combine.

Tasty Moose Pie

Serves 6

There is a virtual cornucopia of recipes available for moose meat, and I believe this has to do with the fact that moose truly is the best of all wild game meats. Moose is a versatile and extremely healthy meat. Probably the most ironic thing about these animals is that many people find them to be the least aesthetically pleasing members of the deer family. With their droopy jowls, elongated nose and huge eyes, they're certainly not the most attractive animal in the woods; but as they always say, you can't judge a book by its cover.

1 cup (250 mL) flour
1 tsp (5 mL) baking powder
1/2 tsp (2 mL) salt
1/2 cup (125 mL) shortening, chunked
1/2 cup (125 mL) mashed potatoes

1 1/2 lbs (680 g) moose steak, cut into 1/4-inch (6 mm) strips
1/2 cup (125 mL) extra-virgin olive oil
1 tsp (5 mL) salt
1/2 tsp (2 mL) pepper
1 cup (250 mL) water

Sift together flour, baking powder and salt in bowl, then cut in shortening. Add mashed potato and mix to form a dough. Chill dough in refrigerator while you prepare meat.

Preheat oven to 300°F (150°C). Coat meat strips in olive oil and season with salt and pepper. Roll up moose strips and place in large casserole dish. Add water. Cook, uncovered, for 1 hour. Roll dough out flat and place it over meat. Return casserole dish to oven and cook for another 20 minutes, until crust is golden brown. Let stand for 5 minutes before serving.

Mexican Moose Pie

Serves 6

The majestic moose can be found in every Canadian province and territory except Prince Edward Island. In some places, they exist in sizeable numbers. In one province in particular, the moose ranges a little more expansively than the rest. Newfoundland boasts the highest density of moose in all of Canada; in fact, there are more moose per square kilometre on "the Rock" than anywhere else in North America. Biologists and the game department continue to work controlling their numbers in the highest growth areas. Hunting and conservation have helped greatly in keeping the moose numbers in Newfoundland under control.

2 Tbsp (30 mL) vegetable oil
1 lb (454 g) ground moose
1 x 12 oz (341 mL) can kernel corn, drained
1 x 7 1/2 oz (213 g) can tomato sauce
1 Tbsp (15 mL) chili powder

1 x 8 oz (318 g) tube refrigerator biscuits
1 cup (250 mL) shredded Cheddar cheese

Preheat oven to 350°F (175°C). Heat oil in large skillet over medium. Cook meat until browned; drain off fat. Stir in corn, tomato sauce and chili powder; keep warm.

For crust, press biscuits onto bottom and up sides of ungreased 9-inch (23 cm) pie plate. Bake for 5 minutes. Spoon moose meat mixture into crust. Sprinkle with cheese. Bake for about 20 minutes, until filling is bubbly and crust is golden brown. Let stand for 5 minutes before serving.

Elk Tenderloin (p. 29)

Summer Moose Brochettes (p. 45)

Moose Meatloaf

Serves 6

Meatloaf lovers out there owe it to themselves to try this recipe. The combination of moose and pork come together for a terrific marriage of flavour and texture. I have tried this recipe with ground moose meat alone; although it is very pleasant, the loaf tends to be a bit dry. By including pork, you are in effect adding a bit of fat and moisture to the concoction. Wild game greenhorns will never know there is moose in this meatloaf, and whether you decide to tell them is strictly up to you. This recipe is every bit as mild as one that includes ground beef.

2 Tbsp (30 mL) butter
1 onion, finely chopped
3 garlic cloves, finely chopped

2 lbs (900 g) ground moose meat
1 lb (454 g) ground pork
3/4 cup (175 mL) bread crumbs
3 eggs, beaten
1/4 cup (60 mL) Worcestershire sauce
3 Tbsp (45 mL) soy sauce
3/4 tsp (4 mL) cayenne pepper
2 tsp (10 mL) salt
1 tsp (5 mL) pepper

Melt butter in medium skillet over medium, then add onion and garlic and sauté for about 5 minutes, until onion is tender.

Meanwhile, in large mixing bowl combine moose meat with remaining ingredients. Add onion mixture and mix well. Coat 9-inch (23 cm) loaf pan with nonstick cooking spray. Spoon meat mixture into loaf pan and level it. Cover with foil and bake for about 1 1/2 hours, until meat is no longer pink in middle. Remove foil, and let meatloaf sit for 5 minutes before serving.

Moose Tacos

Serves 4 to 6

Since much of the country's prime moose hunting areas fall in bear country, protecting your meat from those hungry omnivores can sometimes be a challenge. I remember a story from our old moose camp one evening many years ago, when a quartered moose hanging in the back shed caught the attention of a black bear. The sound of the bear trying to remove the sides of moose from the rack caught the attention of my father and some other members in camp. One of the hunters said, "Is someone not going to scare that bear away?" and the entire camp got up to shoo the bear away just as the bear was dragging one of the large moose quarters down the trail.

2 Tbsp (30 mL) vegetable oil
1 lb (454 g) ground moose
1 envelope taco seasoning mix
1/4 tsp (1 mL) garlic powder

10 taco shells
2 tomatoes, chopped
2 cups (500 mL) shredded lettuce
1 cup (250 mL) shredded Cheddar cheese
sour cream, optional
salsa, optional

Heat oil in large frying pan over medium. Add moose, taco seasoning and garlic powder, and cook for 6 to 7 minutes, until meat is browned.

Spoon meat mixture into taco shells and top with tomato, lettuce, cheese, sour cream and salsa.

Spicy Moose Burgers

Serves 8

The western moose is our second largest moose subspecies and has the widest range in Canada. Found mainly from the Yukon and British Columbia to western Ontario, it also boasts a handful of isolated populations in eastern Canada. The western moose prefers mountainous and highland habitats and exists in limited numbers in Nova Scotia's Cape Breton Highlands, the mountains of New Brunswick and the Chic-Choc Mountains of Québec.

1 lb (454 g) ground moose
1 lb (454 g) ground beef
1 egg
1/4 cup (60 mL) bread crumbs
2 tsp (10 mL) onion powder
1 tsp (5 mL) garlic powder
1/2 tsp (2 mL) pepper
1 Tbsp (15 mL) chopped jalapeño pepper

8 hamburger buns
8 slices Cheddar cheese
8 Tbsp (120 mL) salsa

Preheat grill to medium-high. Combine first 8 ingredients in large bowl and form into 8 equal-sized patties. Grill patties for 8 to 12 minutes, turning occasionally, until just cooked through.

Serve on hamburger buns topped with cheese and salsa.

 Try with This

Sweet Potato Oven Fries

Serves 4

1 tsp (5 mL) seasoned salt
1/2 tsp (2 mL) paprika
1/2 tsp (2 mL) dried parsley
1/4 tsp (1 mL) chili powder
1 1/2 lbs (680 g) sweet potatoes, peeled and cut lengthwise
    into 1/2-inch (12 mm) slices
3 Tbsp (45 mL) olive oil

Preheat oven to 425°F (220°C). In small bowl, combine seasoned salt, paprika, parsley and chili powder. In large bowl, toss sweet potatoes with oil. Sprinkle with seasoning mixture and toss to coat. Arrange sweet potatoes on nonstick baking sheet in single layer. Cook for 40 minutes, until golden brown, turning once.

Moose Jambalaya

Serves 4

Moose Jambalaya is a wild twist on a traditional Cajun meal, and it will appeal to a wide range of dinner guests. Whether you choose the traditional Andouille sausage or spice things up with Merguez sausage, this recipe is sure to please. I always make sure to leave a little bit in the pot for the following day because it keeps well and may be reheated and served as tasty leftovers. You will need to be extra vigilant to not over-simmer this recipe. Moose meat, like most other game, tends to dry out. No more than 20 minutes and you should be good to go.

3 Tbsp (45 mL) butter
1 onion, chopped
1 green pepper, chopped
1 lb (454 g) Andouille or Merguez sausage, chunked

1 x 28 oz (796 mL) can diced tomatoes
1 tsp (5 mL) garlic powder
1/2 tsp (2 mL) salt
1/2 tsp (2 mL) pepper
1 cup (250 mL) cooked moose meat, cut into chunks
1 cup (250 mL) uncooked rice

In large skillet, melt butter and sauté onion, green pepper and sausage for 5 to 7 minutes, until vegetables are tender and sausage has browned slightly.

Add tomatoes, garlic powder, salt, pepper and moose meat and mix. Stir in rice; cover and simmer for about 20 minutes, until rice is tender.

 tip SPECIALTY SAUSAGE

Both Merguez and Andouille sausage can be found in many Canadian supermarkets, especially in the province of Québec. Merguez is more readily available in delis and meat shops across the country, while Andouille sausage will be found in Cajun or French-influenced specialty shops. Ask about them at your local meat counter.

Wild Moose Sausage Patties

Makes about 5 dozen sausages

The moose, as would be expected, produces a fantastic sausage. If any complaint could ever be made about the moose and the various cuts of meat it produces, is that it has almost zero fat content. The main difference in wild game and domestic or commercial meats is the fat running through the tissue and encapsulated within the meat itself, sometimes referred to as "marbling." Wild game meat such as moose, because the animals remain physically active throughout their entire life, do not possess this incorporated layer of fat in the muscle tissue. Any fat found in wild game meats is quickly and easily trimmed away around the circumference.

> 6 lbs (2.7 kg) moose meat, cubed
> 3 lbs (1.4 kg) pork, cubed
> 1/4 cup (60 mL) salt
> 2 Tbsp (30 mL) pepper
> 1 1/2 Tbsp (22 mL) garlic powder
> 1 Tbsp (15 mL) dried crushed chilies
>
> 2 Tbsp (30 mL) vegetable oil

Mix together all ingredients and grind several times. Divide into nine 1 lb (454 g) portions and freeze.

When ready to use, thaw one portion and form into 6 to 8 patties. Heat oil in skillet over medium and cook sausage patties, turning occasionally, until browned and cooked through.

Note: Smoking improves flavour, but sausage may be frozen without smoking.

Smoked Moose Jerky

Makes about 1 lb (454 g) jerky

Probably the best thing about moose jerky, or any jerky, is that it will keep for a long time and can be enjoyed throughout the year. I have great memories of eating moose jerky while sitting in a canoe during the fishing season in May. A big bag of jerky and pepperoni sticks make a great snack for me and the boys. Often when I am preparing lunch during the trout season, I will throw in a few deer pepperoni sticks or a bag of moose jerky on top of the sandwiches.

> 3 lbs (1.4 kg) moose roast
> 3 garlic cloves (wild, if possible), minced
> 2 cups (500 mL) Canadian lager
> 1/4 cup (60 mL) Canadian rye whisky
> 1 cup (250 mL) apple cider vinegar
> 1/2 cup (125 mL) soy sauce
> 3 Tbsp (45 mL) Worcestershire sauce
> 1/4 cup (60 mL) brown sugar
> 1/4 cup (60 mL) salt
> 1/2 tsp (2 mL) onion powder

Cut roast into strips 1/4 inch (6 mm) wide by 1/4 inch (6 mm) thick; the length is not important. Place remaining ingredients in large bowl and mix well. Place meat in bowl and stir to coat. Cover and refrigerate for 24 hours.

Remove meat strips from bowl and place on rack to dry for 2 hours. Be sure to soak wood chips before turning on smoker. Place meat strips in smoker for 14 hours at about 160°F (70°C). Remove jerky from smoker and allow to cool. Store jerky in sealed container or bag.

Weekend Caribou Roast

Serves 8

Because most caribou hunting occurs during late summer, the cold fall temperatures have yet to arrive in the northern tundra. Field dressing and processing the meat, and most importantly cooling it, can be most difficult at this time of year; meat lockers and large cooling devices are not always accessible. Some guides resort to storing caribou meat wrapped in plastic and suspended in the cold water of the northern rivers and lakes—sometimes it's the only way to keep the meat cool.

> 4 lbs (1.8 kg) caribou roast
> 1 envelope onion soup mix
> 1 x 10 oz (284 mL) can condensed cream of mushroom soup
> 1 3/4 cups (425 mL) water
> 8 medium potatoes, peeled and cut in chunks
> 8 carrots, peeled and cut in chunks

Preheat oven to 375°F (190°C). Put roast in roasting pan. Sprinkle onion soup mix over meat. Mix together mushroom soup and water, then pour over meat. Cover. Cook for 2 hours. Add potatoes and carrots. Cook for 1 more hour. Let stand for 5 minutes before serving.

Try with This

Mixed Vegetables

Serves 8

> 1 butternut squash, diced
> 1 yellow pepper, diced
> 1 lb (454 g) green beans, trimmed and cut in half
> 1 carrot, peeled and sliced
> 1/2 cup (125 mL) frozen peas, thawed
> 1 Tbsp (15 mL) butter
> 1 garlic clove, minced
> 1 tsp (5 mL) tarragon
> salt and pepper
> few drops of lemon juice

In medium saucepan over medium-high, boil squash and yellow pepper for about 15 minutes, until tender. Drain and rinse with cold water.

At same time, in small pot over medium-high, boil green beans and carrots for about 10 minutes, until tender. Drain and rinse with cold water. Add peas.

Melt butter in saucepan over medium; add garlic, tarragon and all vegetables. Mix and season to taste with salt, pepper and lemon juice. Heat and serve.

Braised Caribou

Serves 8

Caribou are an icon of the Canadian North and are one of the largest populations of migrating mammals in the world. Known as the reindeer in much of northern Europe, the caribou is a distinctly northern species. Most caribou in Canada are barren-ground caribou, found in large migrating herds in the subarctic of northern Québec, parts of northern Ontario, parts of the Yukon and northern Labrador. They travel muskeg-laden northern regions in search of food and birthing areas. In northern Québec, the George River and Leaf River herds number close to a million animals and are distinctive for their large hooves and wide, sweeping antlers, which are found on both the male and female.

1/2 cup (125 mL) dry red wine
1/2 tsp (2 mL) salt
1/2 tsp (2 mL) pepper
1/4 tsp (1 mL) ground allspice
4 lbs (1.8 kg) caribou roast

1/4 tsp (1 mL) Montréal steak spice
1/2 cup (125 mL) prepared beef broth
1 onion, sliced
4 slices bacon

1 cup (250 mL) blueberry juice

In bowl, combine wine, salt, pepper and allspice. Place roast in heavy-duty resealable plastic bag and pour marinade over roast. Seal bag and refrigerate for 24 hours.

Preheat oven to 350°F (175°C). Remove roast from bag, reserving marinade for later, and place in roasting pan. Sprinkle roast with steak spice. Add broth and onion to pan and place bacon on top of roast. Cook, uncovered, for 1 hour.

Mix together reserved marinade and blueberry juice. Add to roasting pan, cover and cook for 1 additional hour, until roast is slightly pink in centre. Let stand for 5 minutes before serving.

Caribou

Caribou Steak with Mushroom Gravy

Serves 4

Aside from barren-ground caribou, there is another subspecies of caribou in Canada, a much lesser known one called the woodland caribou. It is found in parts of Québec, Ontario, Newfoundland, Labrador and parts of northwestern Canada. The woodland caribou is neither a migrating species, nor does it congregate in large herds, though it does feed on lichens and mosses in the upper boreal forest. Woodland caribou tend to travel in small family groups in more wooded areas as opposed to open tundra.

1/2 cup (125 mL) butter, divided
1 large shallot, finely chopped
1/2 lb (225 g) fresh mushrooms, sliced
1/2 cup (125 mL) prepared beef broth
1 cup (250 mL) heavy cream

2 Tbsp (30 mL) extra-virgin olive oil
4 caribou steaks (sirloin or rib)
1/2 cup (125 mL) flour

Melt 1/4 cup (60 mL) butter in frying pan over medium-high. Sauté shallot and mushrooms for about 5 minutes. Add broth and bring to a boil. Add cream and return to a boil. Reduce heat and simmer until sauce thickens. Cover and remove from heat.

In separate frying pan, heat olive oil and remaining butter. Dredge steaks lightly in flour and place in frying pan. Cook steaks for about 2 to 3 minutes per side, until slightly pink inside. Remove from frying pan and keep warm. To finish your gravy, scrape the drippings from bottom of frying pan and pour sauce in pan. Mix well. Serve over steaks.

Mustard Caribou Steak

Serves 4

The caribou is one of the true symbols of this great country, pictured on the quarter. It is certainly worth your while to try it if you ever get the chance. About 17 years ago, a family friend, Tommy Jones, an experienced caribou hunting guide and conservationist, visited our deer camp and brought a selection of freshly harvested caribou steaks. We sat around camp enjoying Tommy's special caribou meal and listening to stories of the North; it was the most perfect setting for one of my most memorable meals.

4 caribou steaks
salt and pepper
2 Tbsp (30 mL) Dijon mustard
1 tsp (5 mL) prepared horseradish
1 Tbsp (15 mL) vegetable oil

Season steaks with salt and pepper to taste. Combine mustard and horseradish in small bowl and rub mixture all over steaks. Heat oil in large skillet over medium. Place steaks in skillet and cook for 5 to 7 minutes per side, until slightly pink in the middle.

Tender Caribou Steak

Serves 4

When it comes to proper preparation of wild game such as caribou, aging is of utmost importance in producing a good final product. Without an aging process, the various cuts of most red meats would be virtually inedible. Aging promotes tenderness, as the active properties involved in aging help break down fibres in the meat. A general rule of thumb for big game such as caribou, moose and deer is 10 days' hanging time at around 5°C before further processing the meat.

2 Tbsp (30 mL) butter
1/2 cup (125 mL) chopped onion
2 lbs (900 g) caribou sirloin steak
1 cup (250 mL) chopped mushrooms
2 Tbsp (30 mL) flour
1 cup (500 mL) sour cream

(continued on next page)

Melt butter in pan. Add onion and cook for 5 minutes, until soft. Add steaks to pan and sear on both sides. Add mushrooms. In small bowl, stir flour into sour cream and then add to pan. Cover and let simmer for 30 minutes.

Curried Caribou

Serves 4

Although the caribou population in Nord-du-Québec is strong and healthy today, with more than half a million animals in the herd, these animals have seen troubled times in the past. In 1984, a controversial move by Hydro Quebec, where a series of dams were opened to control water levels, resulted in the deaths of over 10,000 caribou that drowned as they crossed the end of the Caniapiscau River as part of their annual migration. A series of fences and migration barriers and walkways were installed to make sure that a mass drowning would never happen again. The estimated population of caribou in 1984 was approximately 300,000 animals, a number which has nearly since doubled thanks to management efforts by several game agencies.

2 Tbsp (30 mL) vegetable oil
1 large onion, chopped
1 tsp (5 mL) minced ginger root
1 tsp (5 mL) ground cumin
3/4 tsp (4 mL) salt
3/4 tsp (4 mL) pepper
1 lb (454 g) caribou meat, cut in bite-sized pieces

2 garlic cloves, minced
1/2 cup (125 mL) water

Heat oil in large cast-iron skillet, and add onion and spices. Stir, then add caribou meat and cook until meat has browned.

Add garlic and water to skillet; simmer gently for about 30 minutes, until meat is tender. Serve with your choice of side.

Canadian Caribou Tenderloin

Serves 4

Caribou are perhaps the most peculiar Canadian ungulates. Not only are they extensively migratory, but they are also a species of the far north and live off a diet of lichens, grasses and other low-growing vegetation. They particularly enjoy eating a moss called old man's beard that grows on black spruce trees. Caribou are equipped with a body dedicated to their migratory habits. They have long, muscular legs and a streamlined body. Perhaps the most unique feature of these northern animals is their huge hoofs, which are shaped in such a way that they act like fins in water. Caribou are the strongest swimmers of all the four-legged creatures in this country.

> 2 lbs (900 g) caribou tenderloin
> 1 cup (250 mL) Canadian lager (or pilsner)
> 1/2 cup (125 mL) vegetable oil
> 1/4 cup (60 mL) Worcestershire sauce
> 1 garlic clove, minced
> 1/2 tsp (2 mL) salt
> 1/2 tsp (2 mL) pepper

Preheat grill to high. Slice caribou tenderloin across the grain into 1-inch (2.5 cm) thick slices. Whisk together beer, oil, Worcestershire sauce and garlic in large bowl. Add tenderloin slices. Stir to coat. Remove meat and reserve sauce. Season slices with salt and pepper to taste, and cook on hot grill, directly over heat, for 2 to 3 minutes per side. Basting the slices with the sauce during grilling will help keep them moist.

Try with This  ## Cucumber Salad

Serves 8

4 English cucumbers, thinly sliced
1 small onion, thinly sliced
1 cup (250 mL) white vinegar
1/2 cup (125 mL) water
3/4 cup (175 mL) sugar
1 Tbsp (15 mL) dried dillweed

Toss together cucumber and onion in large bowl. Combine vinegar, water and sugar in saucepan over medium-high. Bring to a boil. Pour over cucumber and onion. Stir in dill, cover and refrigerate. Serve cold or at room temperature.

Nouveau Québec Stroganoff

Serves 6

Did you know that caribou are the only members of the deer family where both the male and female grow antlers each year? The larger bull caribou shed their antlers in early winter—their racks are more massive and cumbersome and not required once the rut is complete. It is really only the females left with any type of headgear after about mid-December. Some keen thinker determined several years ago that Santa's reindeer, which are basically caribou, must be females because, by Christmastime, the only caribou that still have antlers are the ladies. It certainly makes you wonder...

1 1/2 lbs (680 g) caribou sirloin, cut into 1/2-inch (12 mm) thick slices
1 Tbsp (15 mL) paprika
1/4 cup (60 mL) butter

1 onion, diced
1/2 lb (225 g) mushrooms, sliced
2 cups (500 mL) prepared beef broth
1 Tbsp (15 mL) white vinegar

2 dill pickles, diced
3 Tbsp (45 mL) butter
1/2 tsp (2 mL) salt
1/2 tsp (2 mL) pepper
12 oz (340 g) broad egg noodles, cooked as per package directions

Toss caribou strips in paprika. Melt first amount of butter in skillet on high, then add caribou strips and sear, 2 minutes per side. Take out meat and set aside.

Add onion and mushrooms to skillet, and cook for about 5 minutes, until onion has softened. Add meat, beef broth and vinegar. Simmer for 15 minutes on medium.

Add pickles and second amount of butter. Season with salt and pepper and serve over noodles.

Québec Caribou Tourtière

Serves 8

Growing up in Québec under a strong French Canadian influence, I was exposed to some of the best food in the country. Tourtière was served in our family and in our hotel, the Maplewood Inn, as far back as I remember, but for me it was a bit more of an acquired taste. I jokingly called it "dry pie." As I got older, though, I learned to appreciate the traditional tourtière, especially with caribou meat. It is now something we serve in my family on a regular basis.

> 1 lb (454 g) ground caribou
> 1 lb (454 g) ground pork
> 1 1/2 cups (375 mL) water
> 1 cup (250 mL) diced onion
> 1/2 cup (125 mL) diced celery
> 3/4 tsp (4 mL) salt
> 3/4 tsp (4 mL) pepper
> 1/2 tsp (2 mL) dried rosemary
> 1/2 tsp (2 mL) ground cinnamon
>
> 2 x pastry for 2 crust 9-inch (23 cm) pie
> 1 egg, beaten

In large skillet over high, heat caribou, pork and water until boiling, then add onion, celery, salt, pepper, rosemary and cinnamon. Reduce heat to low then cook, covered, for 1 hour, stirring occasionally. Turn off heat and let cool.

Preheat oven to 400°F (205°C). Line two 9-inch (23 cm) pie plates with pastry. Divide meat mixture equally between pies. Brush egg around outer edge of pastry. Place top crust over each pie and press gently around edge to seal. Trim pastry, crimp edges and cut steam vents in top crusts. Bake for 30 minutes, until crusts are golden brown.

Caribou

Sweet and Sour Caribou Meatballs

Serves 4

The annual barren-ground caribou hunt in Québec is one of the largest conservation efforts in the country. Thanks to several factors that have promoted the growth of the two major Québec caribou herds, the Leaf River herd and the George River herd, the caribou population in Nord-du-Québec has nearly doubled in the last 30 years. The provincial Ministry of Natural Resources establishes caribou hunting in the different zones as a way to control and keep close tabs on the harvest numbers. Things have gone so well that the caribou population continues to increase even with an active late summer hunt. The province has since introduced a winter caribou hunt, which has helped to control the population and increase the harvest of female caribou.

1 lb (454 g) ground caribou
1 egg, beaten
1 onion, diced
1/2 tsp (2 mL) salt
1/2 tsp (2 mL) pepper

1/2 cup (125 mL) canola oil

1 x 14 oz (398 mL) can pineapple chunks
3 Tbsp (45 mL) white vinegar
2 Tbsp (30 mL) sugar
1 Tbsp (15 mL) soy sauce
1 green pepper, diced

Combine meat, egg, onion, salt and pepper in bowl. Roll into 1-inch (2.5 cm) balls.

Heat oil in skillet over high. Add meatballs and brown on all sides. Lower heat, cover and cook for 7 to 10 minutes, until meatballs are cooked through.

Drain pineapple, reserving juice in 2-cup (500 mL) liquid measure. Set pineapple aside. Add enough water to juice to equal 1 1/2 cups (375 mL); pour into saucepan. Stir in vinegar. Add sugar and soy sauce; cook, stirring, over medium for 5 minutes, until thickened. Add meatballs, pineapple and green pepper; cook for another 5 minutes, until heated through and green pepper is soft. Serve hot over egg noodles or white rice.

Hunt Camp Caribou Casserole

Serves 6

Hunt Camp Caribou Casserole is named for its convenience among larger groups of diners; it is often found at hunt camps in fall, whether with caribou or any other type of wild game. Most members of the traditional Canadian hunt camp are fans of wild meat, and dishes such as this one on the menu make life easier during a week of deer, moose or caribou hunting. Regardless whether your camp uses a propane or wood oven, such a casserole can be easily cooked as a main course dinner, then heated up again as leftovers.

3 Tbsp (45 mL) vegetable oil
2 lbs (900 g) minced caribou
1 large onion, diced
2 x 10 oz (284 mL) cans sliced mushrooms, drained
3 wild garlic heads (or 2 regular garlic cloves), minced
2 cups (500 mL) prepared beef broth
2 Tbsp (30 mL) Worcestershire sauce
1/2 tsp (2 mL) pepper

6 cups (1.5 L) hot mashed potatoes
2 cups (500 mL) shredded Cheddar cheese, divided
paprika, sprinkle

Preheat oven to 325°F (160°C). In cast-iron skillet, heat oil. Add caribou and cook until browned. Drain off fat, then add onion, mushrooms, garlic, broth, Worcestershire sauce and pepper. Bring to a boil, reduce heat and simmer for 15 to 20 minutes, until onion is tender.

Pour meat mixture into baking dish. Combine potatoes and 1 cup (250 mL) cheese. Spread over top of meat. Sprinkle with paprika and rest of cheese. Bake, uncovered, for 30 minutes. Let stand for 5 minutes before serving.

Old Veni Stew (p. 16)

Mexican-style Venison Stew (p. 18)

Pronghorn Steak

Serves 4

The pronghorn is a big game animal of Canada's prairies. Pronghorns have a goat-like body with long, prong-shaped horns, as opposed to the antlers most other big game animals have. The unique pronghorn crown continues to grow as the animal ages, producing a sweeping hook at the end as they get older. This prong is their namesake, after all. The current North American pronghorn population ranges between 500,000 and 1 million animals, which is great considering their numbers were down to a mere 20,000 back in the 1920s. Conservation initiatives paid for, in part, by hunters and conservation groups, were responsible for the pronghorn's rebound.

2 Tbsp (30 mL) shortening
4 pronghorn (antelope) steaks, about 1 inch (2.5 cm) thick
1 cup (250 mL) flour
3 cups (750 mL) water, divided

1 x 10 oz (284 mL) can condensed cream of mushroom soup
1 cup (250 mL) diced celery
1 cup (250 mL) sliced mushrooms
1/4 cup (60 mL) diced onion
salt and pepper

Melt shortening in large skillet. Pound steaks in flour and add them to skillet. Brown on both sides. Add 1 1/2 cups (375 mL) water and simmer for 30 minutes.

Add mushroom soup and remaining water. Mix well. Add celery, onion and mushrooms, and salt and pepper to taste. Simmer for 1 hour.

Pronghorn Chili

Serves 6 to 8

In Alberta and Saskatchewan, pronghorns roam in numbers estimated at around 50,000 animals. These migratory beasts have been known to travel up to 5000 miles (8000 kilometres) in a single year. Migration barriers such as the TransCanada Highway are the greatest hurdle facing pronghorns today. In a study that observed one pronghorn attempting to cross the highway, the animal spent 10 days waiting for an opportunity to cross without getting injured. Many localized herds appear to be on the rebound, as conservation of the species focuses on improvements to the migration routes.

3 Tbsp (45 mL) butter
2 lbs (900 g) ground pronghorn
1 large onion, diced
3 garlic cloves, minced
1 x 19 oz (540 mL) can red kidney beans
1 x 14 oz (398 mL) can tomato sauce
1 Tbsp (15 mL) chili powder
1 tsp (5 mL) salt
1 tsp (5 mL) pepper

Melt butter in cast-iron skillet over medium. Add pronghorn, onion and garlic, and cook until meat is browned. Add kidney beans, tomato sauce, chili powder, salt and pepper. Lower heat, cover and simmer for about 1 hour, until mixture thickens. Stir occasionally to prevent sticking.

Try with This  **Alfalfa Sprout Salad**
Serves 6

2 red peppers, thinly sliced
2 green peppers, thinly sliced
3 celery ribs, thinly sliced
2 carrots, thinly sliced
1 cup (250 mL) alfalfa sprouts
1/2 cup (125 mL) French dressing
1 Tbsp (15 mL) prepared mustard

Combine all vegetables in large bowl. In small bowl, combine French dressing and mustard. Stir and pour over vegetables. Mix well and serve.

Pronghorn Meatballs

Serves 6

If you hail from western Canada, there is a good chance you have seen pronghorn sold in specialty game shops, or have been fortunate enough to hunt these animals yourself or know someone who has. Unfortunately, those of us living in central and eastern Canada are not exposed to pronghorn as much as we would like. It is another of our great Canadian red meats, and I am hoping that eventually specialty shops and wild game restaurants in all parts of Canada will carry pronghorn and include it on their menus.

2 lbs (900 g) ground pronghorn
1 cup (250 mL) bread crumbs
1/2 cup (125 mL) diced onion
2 garlic cloves, minced
2 Tbsp (30 mL) soy sauce
1 Tbsp (15 mL) flour
1/2 tsp (2 mL) salt
1/2 tsp (2 mL) pepper

1/4 cup (60 mL) butter

Place everything but butter in large bowl; mix well to combine, and shape into balls about 1 inch (2.5 cm) in diameter.

Heat butter in skillet over medium, then add meatballs. Cook for 5 to 10 minutes, until browned on all sides and firm to the touch. Remove meatballs from pan and serve with any sides you like.

Try with This  **Lentil Salad**

Serves 4 to 6

4 large carrots, sliced
1 x 19 oz (540 mL) can lentils, rinsed and drained
1 celery rib, thinly sliced
1/2 red onion, diced
1/4 tsp (1 mL) salt
1/4 tsp (1 mL) pepper
2/3 cup (150 mL) Italian dressing

In pot over medium, boil carrots for about 15 minutes, until tender. Drain carrots, run under cold water and transfer to large bowl. Add remaining ingredients and mix. Refrigerate for 2 hours before serving.

Tasty Pronghorn Burgers

Serves 8

The pronghorn is a unique animal in Canada, with no close relatives or associated species. Pronghorns are the only big game in Canada with a gall bladder, and they also happen to be the fastest land animals in all of North America, capable of reaching speeds of 80 kilometres per hour. Their great speed is what allows them to escape predators and makes up for the fact that they are very poor jumpers. Pronghorns are most suited to the plains and flatlands of western Canada, where they gather in large groups for protection.

2 lbs (900 g) ground pronghorn
1 onion, diced
1/2 cup (125 mL) water
1/2 cup (125 mL) tomato juice
2 Tbsp (30 mL) ketchup
1 tsp (5 mL) chili powder
1/2 tsp (2 mL) salt
1/2 tsp (2 mL) pepper

2 Tbsp (30 mL) vegetable oil
8 hamburger buns

In bowl, combine pronghorn, onion, water, tomato juice, ketchup, chili powder, salt and pepper. Form into 8 equal-sized patties.

Heat oil in skillet. Add patties and cook for 8 to 12 minutes, turning occasionally, until just cooked through. Serve on hamburger buns with desired toppings.

Try with This  ## Tasty Skillet Mushrooms
Serves 4

1 lb (454 g) fresh mushrooms, sliced
2 Tbsp (30 mL) dry sherry
2 Tbsp (30 mL) butter
1/4 tsp (1 mL) smoked (sweet) paprika
1 tsp (5 mL) seasoned salt
1/8 tsp (0.5 mL) pepper
1/4 cup (60 mL) fresh chopped parsley

In large skillet over medium, combine mushrooms, sherry, butter, paprika, seasoned salt and pepper. Cover and cook for 8 to 10 minutes.

Sprinkle with parsley before serving. Serve with roasted or grilled meat.

Pronghorn Jerky

Makes about 1 lb (454 g) jerky

Only a small proportion of North America's total pronghorn population resides in Canada, and they are limited to southern-most areas of Saskatchewan, Alberta and a small area of British Columbia. In the United States, however, the pronghorn population is estimated at one million animals, stretching out across much of the plains and desert. In the early 1900s, pronghorn numbers were so low that they were faced with extinction. Serious conservation efforts were put into place, and numbers were brought back to where they are now healthy and growing.

> 3 lbs (1.4 kg) pronghorn meat
> 2 Tbsp (30 mL) liquid smoke
> 3 Tbsp (45 mL) water
> 2 tsp (10 mL) pepper
> 1/2 tsp (2 mL) seasoning salt

Slice meat into 1/4-inch (6 mm) thick strips about 4 inches (10 cm) long. Combine liquid smoke, water, pepper and seasoning salt in large bowl. Add meat strips and toss to coat. Cover and refrigerate overnight.

Preheat oven to 175°F (80°C). Remove meat from bowl and pat dry. Place strips across the centre oven rack, allowing space in between. Heat jerky for 10 hours, keeping oven door propped open for last 5 hours. Remove and cool completely. Store in air-tight container.

Easy Bison Breakfast Sausage Patties

Makes about 5 dozen sausages

Sure, you have heard that bison meat is healthy for you, but do you know how healthy bison truly is? When it comes to fat and calorie breakdown, bison has them all beat. It is lower in fat, cholesterol and calories than beef, turkey, chicken and even fish. A typical 3 ounce serving of bison, for example, contains a mere 93 calories, which is composed of a scant 1.8 grams of fat and just 43 milligrams of cholesterol. An equal cut and serving of beef has more than twice as many calories, five times the fat and more cholesterol. It does not take a rocket scientist to figure out that bison is the healthier choice.

5 lbs (2.2 kg) ground bison
3 lbs (1.4 kg) ground pork
2 Tbsp (30 mL) salt
1 Tbsp (15 mL) pepper

2 Tbsp (30 mL) butter

Combine all ingredients. Grind several times through the fine blade of a grinder. Divide into eight 1 lb (454 g) portions and freeze.

When ready to use, thaw one portion and form into 6 to 8 patties. Melt butter in skillet over medium-high and cook sausage patties for 8 to 12 minutes, turning occasionally, until browned and cooked through.

Try with This

Baked Cherry Tomatoes

Serves 6

3 cups (750 mL) cherry tomatoes
2 Tbsp (30 mL) extra-virgin olive oil
1 medium onion, diced
1 to 2 garlic cloves, minced
1/2 cup (125 mL) fresh bread crumbs
1/4 cup (60 mL) chopped fresh parsley
1/4 tsp (1 mL) salt
1/8 tsp (0.5 mL) pepper

Preheat oven to 400°F (205°C). Spray baking dish with nonstick cooking spray and place tomatoes in dish. In small frying pan over medium-high, sauté oil, onion and garlic for 1 to 2 minutes. Add bread crumbs and continue to sauté for another 1 to 2 minutes. Remove from heat and add parsley, salt and pepper. Mix well and spoon over tomatoes. Bake for about 10 minutes, until tomatoes are hot.

Bison Bites

Serves 6 to 8

The once-migratory bison of the prairies have left their mark with long, deep travel paths worn into the ground, which can still be seen from the air today, more than 100 years later. Today's numbers pale in comparison with the estimated population of 50 million back in the mid 1800s, but bison do still roam in Canada, and although they are considered a threatened species, their numbers are stable. There are two main subspecies of bison: the plains bison and the wood bison (or wood buffalo). Thanks to the protection offered by national parks, their numbers are slowly on the rebound.

1/3 cup (75 mL) white vinegar
1/3 cup (75 mL) sesame seeds
1 cup (250 mL) vegetable oil
6 Tbsp (90 mL) soy sauce
1 1/2 tsp (7 mL) garlic powder
1 to 2 Tbsp (15 to 30 mL) dried crushed chilies
1 lb (454 g) bison strip loin or sirloin, cut into
     24 bite-sized pieces

12 slices bacon, halved

Combine first 6 ingredients in large bowl; whisk to blend. Add bison pieces. Toss to coat, then cover and refrigerate for at least 4 hours.

Preheat broiler. Wrap 1 bacon piece around each bison chunk and spear with toothpick. Place bison bites on broiler rack or pan. Cook on lowest rack for about 10 minutes and then move closer to heat and broil for another 5 minutes to crisp the bacon. Serve as an appetizer.

Pictured on page 124.

Bison Sirloin Roast with Cream Sauce

Serves 6 to 8

Bison are raised commercially on quite a large scale in western Canada. They are generally range fed and seem to retain the wild properties passed down through their ancestry. Bison meat is generally regarded as some of the healthiest red meat available on the market today. It is free of additives, extremely high in protein, low in cholesterol and makes a fabulous alternative to beef. This bison sirloin recipe is simply delicious; you will find it tastes very much like beef, with a bit of extra bite.

2 lbs (900 g) bison sirloin roast
1 Tbsp (15 mL) extra-virgin olive oil
1/2 tsp (2 mL) salt
1/2 tsp (2 mL) pepper

4 garlic cloves, minced
1 onion, finely chopped
1 celery rib, finely chopped
1 cup (250 mL) dry white wine
1 cup (250 mL) whole cream

Preheat oven to 350°F (175°C). Coat roast in oil, and season with salt and pepper. Place roast in hot skillet over medium-high, turning to brown all sides. Transfer to a roasting pan and cook for about 1 hour. Remove roast from pan and tent with foil to keep warm.

Place roasting pan on stovetop burner over medium. Add garlic, onion and celery. Cook for 5 to 7 minutes, until vegetables have started to soften, then add wine and cream. Cook for 2 to 3 minutes, until sauce has reduced and thickened. Serve over sliced bison.

Bison

Bison Pepper Steaks

Serves 8

Few people realize that an estimated 20,000 bison in North America do not dwell in a national park or on a ranch and are considered wild. There are two main subspecies of these free-ranging bison. The wood bison tends to be tall and lanky, while their plains cousins are shorter with a more robust body shape. Although increasing in numbers in some areas, bison are still limited by sporadic outbreaks of bovine tuberculosis and brucellosis—diseases brought to North America from Europe in the 1920s.

1 Tbsp (15 mL) whole black peppercorns
1 tsp (5 mL) dill seed
2 tsp (10 mL) paprika
2 tsp (10 mL) hot pepper flakes
1 tsp (5 mL) garlic powder
1/4 tsp (1 mL) salt

4 x 14 to 16 oz (396 to 454 g) bison rib steaks
4 tsp (20 mL) extra-virgin olive oil

Use a mortar and pestle or coffee grinder to grind peppercorns and dill seed together. Place mixture in small bowl with paprika, hot pepper flakes, garlic powder and salt.

Preheat grill to high. Rub each steak with 1 tsp (5 mL) oil and sprinkle with spice mixture. Place steaks on grill and cook with lid closed for 6 to 8 minutes, turning once, until desired doneness.

Pictured on page 87.

 tip **EXTRA-VIRGIN OLIVE OIL**

You may have noticed that many recipes call for extra-virgin olive oil, and you may have wondered—why? When olive oil is made, the most pure variety and that which is intended for human consumption is referred to as "extra virgin." This high-quality oil has a wonderful aroma and adds a subtle sweetness to foods during the cooking process. Extra-virgin olive oil contains antioxidants and is great from a health standpoint. It costs a bit more than regular oil but is worth the expense.

Broiled Bison Steak

Serves 6

The American bison, a symbol of the prairies, is a throwback to this country's past. The bison was once headed for extinction as the great herds in the United States and Canada were almost wiped out in the 19th century. Thanks to the commercial bison farming in this country and some wise management in national parks, bison now exist in solid numbers. If you have ever seen a bison up close, you'll see that it is an extremely impressive animal.

> 6 bison steaks, 1/2 inch (12 mm) thick
> 2 Tbsp (30 mL) vegetable oil
>
> 1/4 cup (60 mL) melted butter
> 1 Tbsp (15 mL) minced onion
> 1/2 tsp (2 mL) salt
> 1/2 tsp (2 mL) pepper

Preheat broiler and brush steaks (from the leg, rib or loin chops of a young animal) with oil; let stand for 15 minutes. Broil steaks 3 inches (7.5 cm) from heat for 7 to 10 minutes per side, making sure they don't get too brown. Remove from oven and let stand for 5 minutes.

Combine butter, onion, salt and pepper; brush on broiled steaks and serve.

Try with This

Skillet Potatoes

Serves 6

2 to 3 lbs (900 g to 1.4 kg) baby potatoes, unpeeled
water to cover

2 Tbsp (30 mL) canola oil
1 Tbsp (15 mL) chopped fresh parsley
1/2 tsp (2 mL) salt
1/2 tsp (2 mL) pepper

Place potatoes in cast-iron skillet and add just enough water to cover potatoes. Place pan on stove burner or grill or over open fire.

Once water has boiled away (approximately 30 minutes), check tenderness of potatoes. If potatoes have not reached desired tenderness, continue to cook in pan until skins are crispy. Drizzle with oil and sprinkle with parsley, salt and pepper.

Buffalo Stir-fry

Serves 4

According to the Canadian Bison Association (CBA), there are an estimated 500,000 bison currently living on farms and ranches throughout North America. In Canada alone, some 250,000 head are owned by nearly 2000 commercial bison producers. With a surge in demand in the 1990s for what the CBA calls "heritage food," the number of bison producers and bison farms grew dramatically. It would appear that Canadians were not only interested in these special creatures as table fare—a national sense of pride was at stake. Now that ranchers, commercial bison farmers, wildlife preserves and national parks all share an interest in bison preservation, their future is all the more bright.

1 egg, beaten
3 Tbsp (45 mL) cornstarch
2 tsp (10 mL) flour
1 lb (454 g) bison steak, cut into strips

3/4 cup (175 mL) sugar
1/2 cup (125 mL) water
1/4 cup (60 mL) apple cider vinegar
1/4 cup (60 mL) soy sauce
1 to 2 Tbsp (15 to 30 mL) cornstarch

3 Tbsp (45 mL) extra-virgin olive oil

2 Tbsp (30 mL) minced ginger root
2 Tbsp (30 mL) minced garlic
2 Tbsp (30 mL) grated carrot

In bowl, mix together egg, first amount of cornstarch and flour. Add bison strips and toss to coat.

In separate bowl, combine sugar, water, vinegar, soy sauce and second amount of cornstarch. Stir and set aside.

Heat oil in deep fryer. Deep-fry meat strips for about 5 minutes. Remove when slightly browned, and drain on paper towel.

In wok, stir-fry ginger, garlic and carrot for about 2 minutes. Stir in soy sauce mixture and cook for about 10 minutes, until thickened. Add meat strips and heat through.

Pictured on page 88.

Bison Chili

Serves 8 to 10

Limiting factors of the bison population in Canada include the threat of depredation by grizzly bears, black bears, wolves and cougars. Much of northern Canada's bison population fortunately does not fall within the normal habitat of these predators. Diseases such as tuberculosis and brucellosis are traditionally seen in cattle but have been known to spread into bison herds. Occasional, though very isolated, breakouts of anthrax have occurred in bison populations, and the risk exists that these diseases may be spread throughout the various bison populations. Fortunately, these animals have a lot of people keeping close tabs on them. Wildlife agencies, park wardens, environmental groups and biologists all play a part in conserving our wild bison populations.

4 Tbsp (60 mL) extra-virgin olive oil, divided
2 medium onions, chopped
2 medium green peppers, chopped
3 lbs (1.4 kg) bison stew meat

5 tsp (25 mL) chili powder
1 Tbsp (15 mL) garlic powder
1 1/2 tsp (7 mL) paprika
1 tsp (5 mL) dried crushed chilies
1/2 tsp (2 mL) Worcestershire sauce
2 x 28 oz (796 mL) cans diced tomatoes
2 x 14 oz (398 mL) cans tomato sauce
2 x 5 1/2 oz (156 mL) cans tomato paste
2 x 14 oz (398 mL) cans red kidney beans
2 x 14 oz 398 mL) cans pinto beans
liquid hot sauce, to taste

Heat 1 Tbsp (15 mL) oil in large Dutch oven. Add onions and green peppers and cook for about 5 minutes, until soft. Meanwhile, heat remaining 3 Tbsp (45 mL) oil in large skillet. Add bison and cook for about 5 minutes, until browned.

Add meat to Dutch oven. Mix in remaining ingredients. Bring to a boil. Reduce heat, cover and simmer for 3 hours. Any leftovers are excellent reheated the next day.

Tasty Bison Meatloaf

Serves 6

The Canadian Bison Association describes the bison farming industry as sustainable agriculture and today's great environmental and economic choice. Canada boasts a population of nearly 200,000 breeding bison cows, and the commercial bison industry can be given credit for this huge number of active animals. Bison ranches are mainly a free ranging or pasture environment. The bison industry works hard at converting formerly cultivated crop land into pasture land. The bison graze on fields where soil erosion is much reduced, and the need for herbicides and pesticides is eliminated.

2 lbs (900 g) ground bison
1/4 lb (115 g) pork sausage
1 cup (250 mL) bread crumbs
1 medium onion, diced
2 celery ribs, diced
2 eggs
1/2 cup (125 mL) chili sauce
1/2 cup (125 mL) tomato juice
1 tsp (5 mL) salt
1 tsp (5 mL) pepper

Preheat oven to 350°F (175°C). Mix together all ingredients in large bowl. Press into greased loaf pan and bake for about 1 1/4 hours, until juices run clear. Serve hot.

Try with This  ## Carrots in Dill Butter

Serves 6

8 carrots, peeled and sliced into 1-inch (2.5 cm) pieces
water to cover

2 Tbsp (30 mL) butter, melted
1 tsp (5 mL) sugar
1/2 tsp (2 mL) salt
1/2 tsp (2 mL) dill seed

Place carrots in medium saucepan and add water to cover. Bring to a boil, then reduce heat and simmer for 25 to 30 minutes, until carrots have reached desired tenderness. Drain.

In small bowl combine butter, sugar, salt and dill seed. Pour over carrots. Stir to coat, and serve hot.

Jalapeño Bison Meatloaf

Serves 6

Anyone who has been up close and personal with a Canadian bison understands what an imposing and regal beast it is. The bison stands no less than 6 feet tall, and its head is about twice the size of a moose's head. I will never forget travelling through Park Omega in Montebello, Québec, a park where the animals roam free and accept offerings from the visitors. This one time, a bison was munching on a carrot I was holding outside my car window when suddenly I was all out of carrot. Oh no, I had no choice but to slowly drive off with the bison's entire head lodged inside of my old Buick Regal. The image of a three-foot long bison head staring me down is something I won't soon forget.

> 2 lbs (900 g) minced bison
> 1/2 tsp (2 mL) pepper
> 1/2 tsp (2 mL) garlic powder
> 3 jalapeño peppers, sliced
> 1 green pepper, sliced
> 3 Tbsp (45 mL) barbecue sauce
> 1 envelope onion soup mix

Preheat oven to 350°F (175°C). Season meat with pepper and garlic powder, then press into loaf pan. Push jalapeño slices into meatloaf. Lay green pepper on top, followed by barbecue sauce. Sprinkle with onion soup mix. Cover and cook on centre rack of oven for 40 minutes. Remove cover and cook for an additional 20 minutes, until meat is cooked through and loaf is dark brown and slightly crispy on top.

Spicy Wild Boar Leg

Serves 6 to 8

The wild boar (also known as a feral pig) is one strange beast. Once popular as an enclosed ranch species, the wild boar now inhabits many parts of the United States and has taken up residence in parts of central and western Canada, where it has learned to adapt to our climate and environment. It travels in small, localized family groups and is pursued by hunters on occasion. The male has large, pronounced tusks. Because the boar is a rooting animal, it can cause a lot of damage to farmlands with its burrowing and digging for food. The meat of the wild boar is delicious and very similar to domestic pork.

1 leg of wild boar
1/2 tsp (2 mL) salt
1/2 tsp (2 mL) pepper
4 cups (1 L) prepared chicken broth

1 cup (250 mL) vegetable oil
1 cup (250 mL) flour
1/2 cup (125 mL) butter
2 cups (500 mL) diced onion
2 cups (500 mL) diced green pepper
2 cups (500 mL) diced celery
3 garlic cloves, minced

1/4 cup (60 mL) diced jalapeno pepper
1 x 28 oz (796 mL) can diced tomatoes
2 x 14 oz (398 mL) cans tomato sauce
1 tsp (5 mL) cayenne

Sprinkle boar leg with salt and pepper. In large skillet over medium-high, brown meat. Add broth and cook on medium for 1 1/2 to 2 hours, until meat is falling off bone. Remove leg from skillet, pick meat off bone, and reserve broth and meat.

Place oil and flour in skillet and cook on high for 5 minutes, constantly stirring. Remove from heat. In separate pan on medium, melt butter and add onion, green pepper, celery and garlic. Cook for about 10 minutes.

Add sautéed vegetables to first skillet. Mix in broth and remaining ingredients. Simmer for 15 minutes, then add meat and simmer for an additional 20 minutes. Let stand for 5 minutes before serving.

Roast Wild Boar

Serves 8

It has only been in the past decade or so that Canadians have come to hear about wild boars roaming freely here. Our neighbours to the south, on the other hand, have been living with these creatures for years. The stories of these sometimes aggressive animals are the stuff of legend in the United States. The male wild boar, which sports long, dangerous tusks as it matures, has been known to charge humans and cause serious injury. People who work in open farmlands in areas in habited by wild boars are mindful of the signs indicating wild boars are near, as are those who hunt the animal.

> 1 x 5 lb (2.2 kg) wild boar roast
> 8 cups (2 L) water
> 3 Tbsp (45 mL) chicken bouillon powder
> 2 x 10 oz (284 mL) cans condensed chicken broth
> 1 tsp (5 mL) garlic powder

1 cup (250 mL) chicken and rib barbecue sauce

Preheat oven to 300°F (150°C). Place roast in roasting pan. Mix together water, bouillon powder, chicken broth and garlic powder. Pour over roast. Place in oven and cook for 4 hours, basting often.

Remove all but 1 cup (250 mL) of liquid from bottom of pan. Pour barbecue sauce over roast, return to oven, reduce heat to 250°F (120°C) and cook for 1 additional hour. Let stand for 5 minutes before serving.

Try with This  ## Cheesy Roasted Potatoes

Serves 8

2 lbs (900 g) potatoes, cut into 1-inch (2.5 cm) chunks
1/2 cup (125 mL) olive oil
1 Tbsp (15 mL) basil
1 Tbsp (15 mL) thyme
2 tsp (10 mL) seasoned salt
1/2 tsp (2 mL) pepper
1 cup (250 mL) grated Parmesan cheese, divided

Preheat oven to 425°F (220°C). Place potatoes in baking dish and drizzle with oil. Sprinkle with basil, thyme, seasoned salt and pepper, and toss to coat. Sprinkle with 1/2 cup (125 mL) of Parmesan cheese and bake for 30 minutes. Remove from oven, stir, and sprinkle on remaining Parmesan cheese. Return to oven for about 30 minutes, until potatoes are tender and browned.

Bison Pepper Steaks (p. 79), Skewered Vegetables on the Grill (p. 163)

Buffalo Stir-fry (p. 81)

Grilled Wild Boar Tenderloin

Serves 4 to 6

Wild boars in Canada are also raised commercially and are range fed, similar to our beef cattle. These commercially raised boars will be slightly different in their consistency and should therefore be cooked in a different manner than a boar taken during hunting. The general rule is that commercially raised livestock tends to be fattier. With wild boar, regardless of the source, lower temperatures and a longer cooking time are the preferred method for flavourful and tender meat. Wild boar tenderloin is very similar to domestic pork tenderloin. Remember, low and slow are the rules of thumb when it comes to tenderloin, and wild boar is no exception.

> 3 garlic cloves, minced
> 1/2 cup (125 mL) orange juice
> 1/4 cup (60 mL) tomato paste
> 2 Tbsp (30 mL) Dijon mustard (with whole seeds)
> 1/2 tsp (2 mL) Worcestershire sauce
> 4 tsp (20 mL) chili powder
> 1 1/2 tsp (7 mL) sugar
> 1 tsp (5 mL) ground cumin
> 1 tsp (5 mL) ground coriander
> 1/4 tsp (1 mL) salt
> 2 wild boar tenderloins

In bowl, combine first 10 ingredients and mix well. Place tenderloins in large resealable plastic bag and pour in marinade. Seal bag and turn to coat. Refrigerate for 2 hours minimum.

Preheat grill to medium-high. Remove tenderloins from bag and place on grill. Close lid; grill, turning regularly, until browned and just a hint of pink remains in the middle. Usually 20 minutes will do it. Let stand for 5 minutes before serving.

Wild Boar Pie

Serves 6

There is not much difference in taste between wild boar and domestic pork. As one would expect from wild meat, boar has a stronger taste and a bit of a wild aroma compared to domestic pork. Wild boar is also leaner than its domestic cousin and therefore lower in fat and cholesterol. Some chefs have described wild boar as being slightly sweeter in taste than domestic pork, but it is often difficult to tell the difference. Keep in mind that pork tends to be a bit difficult to digest as compared to other meats, and moderation is always advised.

2 Tbsp (30 mL) vegetable oil
2 cups (500 mL) diced onions
1 cup (250 mL) diced carrots
1 cup (250 mL) diced celery
3/4 tsp (4 mL) salt
3/4 tsp (4 mL) pepper
2 lbs (900 g) wild boar stew meat, diced
2 Tbsp (30 mL) flour
1 Tbsp (15 mL) tomato paste
1 cup (250 mL) dry red wine
5 cups (1.25 L) prepared beef broth
2 bay leaves
2 sprigs fresh thyme
1 lb (454 g) baby shiitake mushrooms, stems removed

3 cups (750 mL) mashed potatoes
2 Tbsp (30 mL) butter, cubed

Heat oil in large frying pan and add onion, carrot, celery, salt and pepper and cook for 5 to 7 minutes, until vegetables are tender. Add boar meat and cook for an additional 2 minutes. Dust mixture with flour and continue cooking for another 2 minutes, stirring constantly. Stir in tomato paste. Add wine, broth, bay leaves and thyme. Mix well and bring to a boil. Reduce heat and simmer for 1 1/2 hours, until meat is tender, adding mushrooms during last 30 minutes. Pour boar mixture into casserole dish and allow to cool.

Preheat oven to 350°F (175°C). Spread mashed potatoes on top of boar mixture and dot with butter. Place dish in oven and cook for about 30 minutes, until potatoes are slightly browned.

Pictured on page 105.

Wild Boar

Wild Boar Sesame Meatballs

Serves 4

In parts of the Canadian prairies, wild boars have become established as full-time residents. These animals are known to reach enormous, previously unheard of sizes. I recently read about a wild boar taken by a hunter in Saskatchewan that weighed in excess of 400 pounds (180 kg), making it as large as some grizzly bears. The fact that wild boars are capable of reaching these enormous sizes is a testament to their adaptability. The boar populations that exist across Canada have fought their way into existence by being able to forage for food in the wild and cope with our harsh winter conditions.

1 lb (454 g) ground wild boar
1 garlic clove, minced
1 green onion, chopped
2 Tbsp (30 mL) soy sauce
1 Tbsp (15 mL) roasted sesame seeds
1/4 tsp (1 mL) pepper

1/2 cup (125 mL) flour
1 egg, beaten with 1 Tbsp (15 mL) water
2 Tbsp (30 mL) vegetable oil

1/4 cup (60 mL) soy sauce
1/4 cup (60 mL) white vinegar
2 tsp (10 mL) honey
1/2 tsp (2 mL) hot pepper sauce
2 tsp (10 mL) roasted sesame seeds

In bowl, mix together ground boar, garlic, green onion, soy sauce, first amount of sesame seeds and pepper. Shape mixture into 1 1/2-inch (4 cm) diameter meatballs.

Place flour in one bowl and egg mixture in separate bowl. Roll each meatball in flour, then in egg mixture and then again in flour. Heat oil in skillet over medium. Drop meatballs into skillet and fry for 10 to 15 minutes, until cooked.

While meatballs are cooking, combine all remaining ingredients and mix well to make a dipping sauce. Serve with meatballs.

Bountiful Bear Roast

Serves 6 to 8

There are three species of bear found in North America: the polar bear, the grizzly bear and the black bear. The polar bear is found only in the Arctic regions, with their southern limit determined by sea ice pack. The grizzly bear is an animal of western Canada, the northwestern United States and Alaska. In the mountainous areas of the Yukon, Alberta and British Columbia, the grizzly bear dwells in sizable numbers. Black bears are the most ubiquitous of all bears, with their range extending all across Canada and through more than half of the United States. Black bears are also the smallest bears and, contrary to their name, range from black to honey brown in colour. Bears are magnificent and perhaps the toughest and most resilient animals in the country.

1 x 2 to 3 lb (900 g to 1.4 kg) bear roast
1/2 tsp (2 mL) salt
1/2 tsp (2 mL) pepper
1 garlic clove, minced

1 cup (250 mL) tomato juice
1/2 cup (125 mL) water
1/4 cup (60 mL) ketchup
1/4 cup (60 mL) white vinegar
2 Tbsp (30 mL) Worcestershire sauce
2 Tbsp (30 mL) brown sugar
1 Tbsp (15 mL) paprika
1/2 tsp (2 mL) salt
1/2 tsp (2 mL) pepper
1/4 tsp (1 mL) chili powder
1/8 tsp (0.5 mL) cayenne pepper

Preheat oven to 350°F (175°C). Place roast in roasting pan, season with garlic and first amounts of salt and pepper, and cook for 1 hour.

In skillet, combine remaining ingredients. Mix well and heat over medium. Simmer for 15 minutes. Slice roast into thin slices and add to skillet. Simmer for 1 additional hour, or until meat is tender. Let stand for 5 minutes before serving.

Bear

Slow Cooker Bear Roast

Serves 6 to 8

The black bear is the most common, and therefore most commonly eaten, bear in Canada. Depending on the province, there may be a fall or spring hunting season. In central Canada, Québec relies mostly on the spring bear season, while Ontario maintains a bear season in fall. From a consumption standpoint, some people feel that the meat of a spring bear is better. One reason may be that the bears that emerge from hibernation in spring are very lean from their long period of dormancy. Fall bears tend to be fatty because they have been gorging themselves in preparation for hibernation.

3/4 cup (175 mL) extra-virgin olive oil
3/4 cup (175 mL) dry red wine
2 Tbsp (30 mL) Italian seasoning
1 x 2 to 3 lb (900 g to 1.4 kg) bear roast

1/2 tsp (2 mL) garlic powder
1/2 tsp (2 mL) salt
1/2 tsp (2 mL) pepper
1 Tbsp (15 mL) extra-virgin olive oil

1 lb (454 g) fresh baby carrots, sliced
6 large potatoes, peeled and cut into chunks
1 x 10 oz (284 mL) can mushroom stems and pieces, drained

1 x 10 oz (284 mL) can condensed cream of mushroom soup
1 x 10 oz (284 mL) can beef gravy
1 cup (250 mL) water
1 envelope onion soup mix

In large resealable plastic bag, combine first amount of olive oil, wine and Italian seasoning. Add bear roast, seal bag, and turn to coat. Refrigerate for 24 hours.

Remove meat from bag, drain and pat dry. Season roast with garlic powder, salt and pepper. Heat second amount of olive oil in large skillet over medium-high. Cook roast for about 8 minutes, making sure to sear all sides.

Place carrots, potatoes and mushrooms in slow cooker. Place meat on top of vegetables.

In bowl, combine soup, gravy, water and onion soup mix. Mix well and pour over roast in slow cooker. Cook on Low for 6 hours, or until meat is tender. Serve bear roast and vegetables with gravy spooned over each serving.

Bear Steaks

Serves 4

Bear meat, whether black bear or grizzly bear, has a very distinct flavour and texture. It is a rich red meat with an almost pork-like taste. Cooking bear meat, however, requires caution. Undercooked bear is famous for the spread of a disease called trichinosis. Although bear meat may be more tender when cooked to medium-rare, it is imperative that any bear you serve is cooked well. When the meat is well cooked, there is zero chance of contracting this disease, and it still tastes great.

> 2 Tbsp (30 mL) vegetable oil
> 2 lbs (900 g) bear steak, cut in thin strips
> 2 onions, cut into rings
>
> 1 x 10 oz (284 mL) can condensed cream
>   of mushroom soup
> 3/4 cup (175 mL) dry sherry
> 1 x 10 oz (284 mL) can sliced mushrooms,
>   drained (reserve liquid)
> 2 garlic cloves, minced

Heat oil in cast-iron skillet over high, and place steak strips in skillet. When meat has started to brown, add onion rings and cook for 5 minutes, until tender.

In bowl, combine soup, sherry, reserved mushroom liquid and garlic, and pour over steaks in skillet. Add mushrooms, cover, reduce heat and simmer for approximately 1 hour, until steak is tender.

Bear Stew

Serves 8

Of all North American game animals, bear is perhaps the most underused. Because bears are omnivores, some foodies and others in the culinary arts tend to discount their meat as palatable. The old adage, "I don't eat animals that eat other animals" tends to give this fine game meat a bad rap. When bear is prepared with care and cooked properly, it is not only extremely safe, but it is also extremely tasty. This mild, flavourful bear stew is a terrific option for those who wish to disguise any natural game flavouring. Give bear meat a chance, and you may just surprise yourself.

1/4 cup (60 mL) flour
1 tsp (5 mL) dried oregano
1 tsp (5 mL) salt
1 tsp (5 mL) pepper
4 lbs (1.8 kg) bear meat, cut into 1-inch (2.5 cm) cubes
1/4 cup (60 mL) butter
2 Tbsp (30 mL) extra-virgin olive oil

2 to 3 qts (2 to 3 L) water
1 cup (250 mL) prepared beef broth
2 lbs (900 g) potatoes, chopped
1 lb (454 g) fresh mushrooms, sliced
1 onion, chopped
5 carrots, chopped
2 turnips, chopped
4 bay leaves

In large bowl, combine flour, oregano, salt and pepper. Place bear meat in bowl a little at a time, stirring to coat well. In large skillet over medium-high, heat butter and oil until melted. Add bear meat and cook until browned. Drain meat on paper towels.

Place water in large Dutch oven. Add bear meat and remaining ingredients. Cook on medium-high for 2 to 3 hours. Serve with crusty bread or French baguette.

Bear Casserole

Serves 4

The black bear is one of the most respected and feared animals on earth. It is amazing how one beast can garner such a reputation as a blood thirsty creature based on a few isolated encounters. The fact is, compared to the number of people attacked by domestic dogs in this country, the number of bear attacks pales in comparison. Sure, there are a handful of bear encounters each year in Canada, and occasionally a small number of them prove to be fatal, but these events are the exception rather than the rule. The black bear is a dangerous animal with the potential to be lethal, but understanding the biology and behaviour of this species and being prepared while travelling in the woods can make all the difference.

> 2 Tbsp (30 mL) vegetable oil
> 1 lb (454 g) bear meat, cut into 1-inch (2.5 cm) cubes
> 1/2 cup (125 mL) flour
>
> 1/2 cup (125 mL) water
> 1 onion, diced
> 1 tsp (5 mL) garlic powder
> 1/2 tsp (2 mL) salt
> 1/2 tsp (2 mL) pepper

Preheat oven to 350°F (175°C). Heat oil in cast-iron skillet. Dredge meat cubes in flour and place in skillet to brown. Transfer meat to baking pan.

Add remaining ingredients, cover and cook for 1 hour.

Try with This  ## Mashed Carrots and Turnips
Serves 8

> 1 lb (454 g) carrots, peeled and cut into
>   1-inch (2.5 cm) pieces
> 1 lb (454 g) turnips, peeled and cut into
>   1-inch (2.5 cm) pieces
> 1/4 cup (60 mL) butter
> 1/4 cup (60 mL) cream (optional)
> 1/2 tsp (2 mL) salt
> 1/2 tsp (2 mL) pepper

In large pot, boil carrots and turnips, covered, for about 30 minutes, until soft. Drain. Add butter and mash until consistency of lumpy mashed potatoes. Add cream for a creamier texture. Season with salt and pepper.

Bear Meatloaf

Serves 6

The black bear is the widest ranging of the three bear species in Canada. It is found in every province and territory except Prince Edward Island. Black bears are omnivores; their diet consists mostly of berries and grasses, supplemented with small mammals, deer and, during spring, young moose calves. In several provinces, black bears are responsible for upward of 30 percent of moose calf mortality. The black bear is an often-misunderstood animal and, as with its larger western cousin, the grizzly bear, it can be quite unpredictable. When you travel in bear country, vigilance is always required as attacks on humans, though rare, occur every year.

> **2 lbs (900 g) ground bear**
> **1 cup (250 mL) bread crumbs**
> **2 eggs**
> **3/4 cup (175 mL) tomato sauce**
> **1/2 cup (125 mL) milk**
> **1 cup (250 mL) diced onion**
> **1/2 green pepper, diced**
> **1 1/2 tsp (7 mL) dry mustard**
> **1/2 tsp (2 mL) salt**
> **1/2 tsp (2 mL) pepper**
> **1/4 tsp (1 mL) ground thyme**

Preheat oven to 350°F (175°C). In large bowl, combine all ingredients and mix well. Place mixture in loaf pan and bake for about 1 hour, until cooked through. Cut through centre to check for doneness.

Quick Bear Meatballs

Serves 6

Each fall, in Arundel, Québec, my late uncle would hold a popular Hunter's Supper at his steakhouse, Alfred's Beefeater. His chef would serve a variety of game meats including moose, deer and an assortment of wild fowl. One fall, he introduced bear to the menu. It piqued the curiosity of many a restaurant patron, as bear was not a usual addition to the Beefeater menu. I was fortunate enough to be there that evening and am pleased to report that the bear was exceptional and the uniqueness of the flavours was a real treat. I can remember Uncle Alfie explaining to me how he thought this bear was very similar to pork, and he was right, there was a hint of pork and it was rather tasty.

2 lbs (900 g) ground bear
1/2 cup (125 mL) bread crumbs
1/4 cup (60 mL) chopped onion
2 Tbsp (30 mL) milk
2 Tbsp (30 mL) vegetable oil
2 Tbsp (30 mL) flour
1 1/2 cups (375 mL) water

Mix together meat, bread crumbs, onion and milk in large bowl. Form into 1 1/2-inch (4 cm) diameter balls. Heat oil in frying pan. Add meatballs and cook until browned. Add flour and water to make gravy, and simmer for 1 hour.

Try with This  ## Cooked Sweet Beets

Serves 6

2 x 14 oz (398 mL) cans sliced beets, drained
1/2 cup (125 mL) liquid honey
1/4 cup (60 mL) lemon juice
1 tsp (5 mL) grated lemon zest
1/2 tsp (2 mL) salt
1/4 tsp (1 mL) ground nutmeg
2 Tbsp (30 mL) butter

Preheat oven to 350°F (175°C). Layer beets in casserole dish. In small bowl, mix together honey, lemon juice, zest, salt and nutmeg. Pour honey glaze over beets, and dot with butter. Cook in oven for 20 to 30 minutes.

Apple Rabbit

Serves 4 to 6

Rabbits are both raised commercially for eating and hunted in the wild across Canada. As expected, commercial rabbits are a bit fattier than those taken from the wild. Chefs will often soak or marinate rabbits in salt water overnight to take away some of the gaminess in the meat. For most wild game, a good marinade can often minimize the gamey taste as well as add some moisture to the meat. Rabbit is very low in cholesterol compared to chicken and is lower in calories as well. Though it is eaten only occasionally in Canada, other parts of the world such as Europe and Australia include rabbit as part of their regular diet.

2 Tbsp (30 mL) vegetable oil
1 rabbit, cleaned, cut up into pieces
1 cup (250 mL) flour (for dusting)
1/2 tsp (2 mL) salt
1/2 tsp (2 mL) pepper

4 slices bacon, cut into pieces
4 onions, chopped
2 lbs (900 g) apples, peeled, cored and chopped
2 1/2 cups (625 mL) apple cider

Preheat oven to 325°F (160°C). Heat oil in large skillet over medium. Dust rabbit pieces with flour, season with salt and pepper, and place in skillet. Cook until browned and then transfer to bowl and set aside.

In same skillet, fry bacon and onions until golden brown. Add apples and cook for 3 to 5 more minutes. Add meat. Season to taste with additional salt and pepper, then pour in apple cider. Bring to a boil. Transfer mixture to casserole dish. Cover and then transfer to oven. Cook for 1 hour, or until rabbit is tender. Let stand for 5 minutes before serving.

Pictured on page 106.

Mustard Rabbit Casserole

Serves 4 to 6

The cottontail rabbit and snowshoe hare are Canada's most common members of the rabbit family. They are small, muscular animals, with two sets of pronounced incisors and fully furred feat, and when cooked properly can provide fabulous table fare. Because much of the wild rabbit is dark meat, with a somewhat more distinct and bold flavour than farmed rabbit, it does not appeal to everyone. However, this great Mustard Rabbit Casserole recipe will allow almost everyone to enjoy rabbit.

1 Tbsp (15 mL) flour
1 Tbsp (15 mL) dry mustard
1 rabbit, cleaned, cut up into pieces
3 Tbsp (45 mL) vegetable oil

6 Tbsp (90 mL) butter, divided
1 onion, sliced
2/3 cup (150 mL) apple cider
1 1/4 cups (300 mL) prepared chicken broth
1 Tbsp (15 mL) white vinegar
1 Tbsp (15 mL) sugar
1 Tbsp (15 mL) prepared mustard
3/4 tsp (4 mL) sal3/4 tsp (4 mL) pepper

1/4 cup (60 mL) bread crumbs

In bowl, combine flour and dry mustard. Coat rabbit pieces in flour mixture; reserve any remaining flour mixture. Heat oil in large skillet and add rabbit. Cook until browned. Transfer to casserole dish or baking pan.

Preheat oven to 350°F (175°C). In separate skillet, melt 2 Tbsp (30 mL) butter. Add onion and cook for 5 minutes, until tender. Add reserved flour mixture and cook for 1 minute. Gradually add cider and broth; bring to a gentle boil. Add vinegar, sugar and mustard; stir well. Season with salt and pepper. Pour mixture over rabbit in casserole and cook in oven, uncovered, for about 60 minutes, until tender.

In skillet over medium-high, melt remaining 4 Tbsp (60 mL) butter. Add bread crumbs. Cook until golden brown. Sprinkle bread mixture on top of cooked rabbit and let stand for 5 minutes before serving.

Hunt Camp Hare

Serves 6 to 8

At our camp, when it comes to meals for the guys, the task of cooking is usually divided between my father and me, and we usually stick to the basics. On top of the meals that we serve for the group, however, each member is also responsible for one meal of their own. Sometimes we get hung up on tradition, too often falling back on the tried-and-true venison, moose, duck and grouse dishes, when there is a virtual cornucopia of other choices out there, including rabbit. Watch out boys, and get ready for Hunt Camp Hare.

1 cup (250 mL) flour
2 x 2 lb (900 g) hares, cleaned, cut up into pieces
1/4 cup (60 mL) vegetable oil
2 Tbsp (30 mL) butter

1 cup (250 mL) chopped onion
1 garlic clove, minced
1 Tbsp (15 mL) flour
2 tsp (10 mL) salt
1/4 tsp (1 mL) pepper
1 cup (250 mL) milk

1 cup (250 mL) sour cream

Preheat oven to 350°F (175°C). Place first amount of flour in bowl and dredge rabbit pieces. Heat oil and butter in medium oven-proof skillet over medium-high. Add rabbit and cook until browned on all sides. Remove pieces to platter as they are browned.

Lower heat to medium, and in drippings in skillet, cook onion and garlic for about 5 minutes, until tender. Stir in second amount of flour, salt and pepper. Gradually stir in milk and cook, stirring constantly, for 10 to 12 minutes, until mixture thickens. Return rabbit pieces to skillet; spoon sauce over pieces.

Cover and cook in oven for 1 hour and 10 minutes, or until rabbit is fork-tender. Remove pieces to warm platter. Stir sour cream into gravy; heat, stirring constantly, until hot (do not boil). Serve gravy over rabbit.

Old-school Rabbit Stew

Serves 4 to 6

Commercially raised rabbits and hares are almost entirely composed of white meat, which stems from their sedentary lifestyle. Wild rabbits, by contrast, are almost all dark meat. No matter the type or species of rabbit, stew is perhaps the most universal way of serving the small mammal. After the simmering is complete, a combination of vegetables and rabbit meat will blend together for a very tasty and hearty dish. It is one meal sure to please the stew lovers in your family.

> 3 Tbsp (45 mL) vegetable oil
> 1 rabbit, cleaned, cut up into pieces
> 1 Tbsp (15 mL) beef bouillon powder
> 2 cups (500 mL) water
> 3/4 tsp (4 mL) salt
> 3/4 tsp (4 mL) pepper
>
> 1 medium onion, chopped
> 3 medium carrots, chopped
> 5 medium potatoes, chopped
> 1 medium turnip, chopped
>
> 1/4 cup (60 mL) flour
> 1/4 cup (60 mL) water
> 1 garlic clove, minced

Heat oil in large Dutch oven. Add rabbit pieces and cook until lightly browned. Dissolve bouillon powder in first amount of water, and add salt and pepper. Pour over meat in Dutch oven and cover. Simmer on low for 2 hours, or until rabbit meat is starting to tenderize.

Add vegetables to Dutch oven and simmer, covered, for another 45 minutes, or until vegetables are tender.

In small bowl, combine flour, second amount of water and garlic, and add to stew. Stir gently, uncovered, until sauce is slightly thickened. Serve immediately.

Hare Bourguignon

Serves 4

During most years in the southern and central regions of Canada, the snowshoe hare is an extremely plentiful small game animal. The lifecycle of the snowshoe hare is very dependent on the predator/prey relationship. The populations of such predators as the lynx, bobcat, coyote and timber wolf have a significant effect on the hare population in Canada. Hare populations are typically cyclical, with years of high numbers followed by years of very low numbers of animals.

3/4 cup (175 mL) dry red wine
6 to 8 whole peppercorns
1 bay leaf
4 snowshoe (or European) hare legs, skinned and rinsed

1/4 cup (60 mL) flour
4 slices bacon, cut into 1-inch (2.5 cm) pieces

1 cup (250 mL) prepared chicken broth
2 cups (500 mL) sliced mushrooms
1 medium onion, chopped
1 garlic clove, minced
1 tsp (5 mL) dried thyme

1 Tbsp (15 mL) butter, softened
1 Tbsp (15 mL) flour

Place red wine, bay leaf and peppercorns in large bowl; add hare legs. Cover and refrigerate for minimum 3 hours or overnight.

Remove hare legs from bowl, reserving marinade. Cover legs evenly with first amount of flour. Cook bacon in Dutch oven over medium-high for 10 to 15 minutes, until crisp. Remove bacon and drain all but 2 Tbsp (30 mL) bacon fat. Add legs to bacon fat in Dutch oven and cook for about 10 minutes, browning all sides.

Add reserved marinade and broth, mushrooms, onion, garlic and thyme, and stir well. Cover and bring to a boil; reduce heat and simmer for 30 minutes.

Mix butter and second amount of flour to form a paste. Gradually add to stew, stirring. Return bacon to Dutch oven and bring mixture to a boil. Cook for 5 to 7 minutes, until sauce thickens. Serve immediately.

Sweet and Sour Rabbit

Serves 6

This Asian-influenced recipe is my favourite when it comes to serving rabbit for dinner. Although there are many ways to cook rabbit, for some reason, the sweet and sour style is one that really does it justice. This recipe is also good for people who have an aversion to dark meat, as most wild rabbit is composed of dark meat. This tasty dish can be served on a variety of occasions.

> 1 cup (250 mL) flour
> 1 whole rabbit, cleaned, cut up into pieces
> 2 Tbsp (30 mL) vegetable oil
>
> 1 cup (250 mL) pineapple juice
> 1/4 cup (60 mL) white vinegar
> 1/2 tsp (2 mL) salt
>
> 1 cup (250 mL) chopped pineapple
> 1 medium green pepper, thinly sliced
>
> 1 1/2 Tbsp (22 mL) cornstarch
> 1/2 cup (125 mL) water

Place flour in bowl and roll meat pieces in it to cover completely. In large skillet over medium, heat oil and add rabbit pieces. Cook until browned.

Add pineapple juice, vinegar and salt to skillet; cover. Simmer on low for approximately 40 minutes.

Add pineapple and green pepper, and cook for an additional 5 minutes.

In liquid measuring cup, combine cornstarch and water; mix well. Pour cornstarch mixture into skillet gradually; continue to heat until sauce has thickened, approximately 5 minutes. Serve immediately.

Wild Boar Pie (p. 90)

Apple Rabbit (p. 99)

Hare with Sweet Sauce

Serves 8 to 10

Hare hunters in Canada most commonly pursue the snowshoe hare in early fall because our weather conditions often play tricks on this rabbit. It is alternatively named the varying hare because its colour changes throughout the year. In late summer, the snowshoe will begin to develop a whiter coat. By the time winter arrives, the coat will match almost perfectly its snowy surroundings. During fall, however, an early snowfall can prompt the snowshoe hare to change colour more quickly; and if a stretch of warm weather ensues, the now all-white hare stands out in the forest like a sore thumb, making it an easier target for hunters.

> **2 rabbits, cleaned, cut into quarters**
> **cool water to cover**
> **1/2 cup (125 mL) white vinegar, divided**
> **2 tsp (10 mL) salt**
> **1 onion, chopped**
> **4 whole cloves**
> **1/2 cup (125 mL) dark raisins**
> **1/4 cup (60 mL) brown sugar**
>
> **3 to 4 Tbsp (45 to 60 mL) flour**

Place rabbit pieces in deep pot and cover with cool water. Add 1/4 cup (60 mL) vinegar and bring to a boil. Boil for 5 minutes; discard water. Again, cover rabbit with cool water and add remaining vinegar, salt, onion and cloves. Cook for 5 minutes, until almost tender, and then add raisins and brown sugar. Continue cooking for another 10 minutes, until rabbit is tender and done.

Remove rabbit from pot and thicken sauce by adding flour 1 Tbsp (15 mL) at a time until desired consistency. Replace rabbit in pot and heat just before serving.

Marinated Slow Cooker Hare

Serves 4 to 6

I grew up in the mountains of Québec, where hare is often served. Since many people hunted and trapped snowshoe hares, and used them to feed their families, it was common to see these animals out hanging from the clotheslines in towns north of Montréal in winter. As with other game meats, hare meat that has been properly hung and aged will be more tender and tasty than meat that has not been hung long enough.

3 cups (750 mL) water
1/2 cup (125 mL) white vinegar
2 garlic cloves, minced
2 Tbsp (30 mL) salt
1 rabbit, cleaned, cut up into pieces

2 Tbsp (30 mL) oil
1 large onion, chopped
2 celery ribs, chopped
2 carrots, chopped
1 green pepper, chopped
1 cup (250 mL) dry white wine
3 Tbsp (45 mL) tomato paste
1/2 tsp (2 mL) cayenne pepper

Place first 4 ingredients in large bowl. Add rabbit, cover and refrigerate for 12 hours.

Remove rabbit and pat dry. Heat oil in skillet over medium-high and add rabbit, onion, celery, carrots and green pepper. Cook for 5 to 10 minutes, until rabbit is browned. Transfer mixture to slow cooker and add remaining ingredients. Cover and cook on Low for 8 to 10 hours.

Rabbit on the Grill

Serves 4 to 6

This rabbit recipe is the perfect choice for an outdoor cooking session. If you are familiar with my *Canadian Outdoor Cookbook*, you will know that many different techniques are available for cooking on the grill, and that there are a variety of techniques for serving up a great wild bounty, including rabbit and hare. An outdoor grill provides a smoky flavour when using a natural wood fire, and those flavours translate perfectly to the meat. Your grilled rabbit done on an outdoor grill or open fire, might be the best you have ever had.

1 rabbit, cleaned, cut up into pieces
1/2 cup (125 mL) lemon juice

3/4 cup (175 mL) butter
2 tsp (10 mL) salt
2 tsp (10 mL) dried savory
1 tsp (5 mL) paprika
1 tsp (5 mL) dry mustard
1/4 tsp (1 mL) pepper

Place rabbit in bowl and pour lemon juice over it. Cover and refrigerate for at least 3 hours.

Preheat grill to low. Remove rabbit from bowl and pat dry. In small saucepan, melt butter and add remaining ingredients. Brush rabbit with butter mixture and place on grill. Cook, brushing frequently, for about 40 minutes, until golden brown and tender.

Try with This 
Potatoes and Onions on the Grill

Serves 4

4 medium potatoes
1 onion
1/4 cup (60 mL) butter, cut into 1-inch (2.5 cm) by 1/4-inch
   (6 mm) slices
1 tsp (5 mL) Montréal steak spice
1/4 cup (60 mL) sour cream, optional

Preheat grill to high. Cut potatoes into slices about 1/4 inch (6 mm) thick, but only about 3/4 through each potato; potatoes should be held together at bottom. Cut onion into thinner slices. Place onion slices between potato slices and top with small pieces of butter. Sprinkle steak spice on top and wrap each potato in heavy-duty foil to form little packets. Cook for about 30 minutes, turning occasionally. Serve with sour cream if you desire.

Muskrat Chili

Serves 6

For those of you who are a bit squeamish when it comes to game meats, I am here to tell you that the more fringe meats such as muskrat and beaver could very well surprise you. It is common knowledge among outdoorsmen that the flesh of the beaver and the muskrat is delectable and as flavourful as any other red meat. People who live off the fat of the land, who hunt and gather their food, have been enjoying muskrat for centuries. If you have a trapper in the family, next winter, do yourself a favour and try one of these recipes featuring our Canadian furbearers.

> 2 lbs (900 g) muskrat meat, cut into 1-inch (2.5 cm) cubes
> 1/2 tsp (2 mL) garlic powder
> 1/2 tsp (2 mL) pepper
>
> 3 Tbsp (45 mL) extra-virgin olive oil
> 1 large onion, chopped
> 4 carrots, diced
> 6 celery ribs, chopped
> 3 garlic cloves, minced
>
> 1 x 28 oz (796 mL) can diced tomatoes
> 1 x 14 oz (398 mL) can tomato sauce
> 1/2 tsp (2 mL) chili powder

Season muskrat with garlic powder and pepper. Set aside.

Heat oil in cast-iron skillet over medium-high. Add onion, carrots, celery and garlic and cook for 5 to 7 minutes, until softened. Add meat; cover and cook for 10 minutes.

Add tomatoes, tomato sauce and chili powder. Bring to a boil, and then reduce heat, cover and simmer for 1 hour. Serve with fresh bread.

Slow Cooker Muskrat Stew

Serves 6

Muskrat meat is, simply put, one of the most delicious meats you will find in the wild. The greatest difficulty in serving muskrat is that these animals are fur bearers and must be taken through legal trapping methods as opposed to hunting, so gaining access to muskrat and beaver for table purposes is difficult. If you should happen to get some fresh muskrat, another small hurdle is being able to trim the meat from these small mammals. The best meat for this stew is around the hind quarters and legs. It must be trimmed away in small pieces, after skinning it of course. As with other wild game, you will notice that muskrat contains very little fat or sinew.

> 1 cup (250 mL) flour
> 1/2 tsp (2 mL) salt
> 1/2 tsp (2 mL) pepper
> 3 cups (750 mL) muskrat meat, cut into
>   1-inch (2.5 cm) cubes
> 3 Tbsp (45 mL) extra-virgin olive oil
> 1 medium onion, chopped
> 1 cup (250 mL) diced carrots
> 1 cup (250 mL) cubed potatoes
> 1 cup (250 mL) cubed turnip
> water, to cover

Place flour, salt and pepper in large bowl. Add muskrat meat and toss to coat. Heat oil in cast-iron skillet over medium-high. Add muskrat and cook until browned. Transfer meat to slow cooker. Add onion, carrots, potatoes and turnips. Add enough water to cover. Cook on Low for 5 hours, or until veggies are tender.

Fried Beaver Pepper Steaks

Serves 8 to 10

One of my fondest memories as a child is of travelling with my father on snowmobile from our hotel in the Laurentians to check on his active trap line. My father and I would pursue beavers and fishers and spend long hours out in the mountains near our camp. That one winter, after travelling to a distant beaver pond, we hit pay dirt with six adult beaver, which needed to be carried back to the snowmobile. I was barely nine years old, so the animals had to be skinned on site to reduce the weight. The process took several hours, and I started to get hungry. My father built a fire and cooked up a couple of delicious beaver steaks. It was a moment I will never forget.

> 1 lb (454 g) bacon, chopped
>
> 1 cup (250 mL) flour
> 1/2 tsp (2 mL) garlic powder
> 1/2 tsp (2 mL) pepper
> 1 tsp (5 mL) Montréal steak spice
> 3 lbs (1.4 kg) beaver steaks, from hind legs
> 1/2 cup (125 mL) sliced mushrooms
> 1 large onion, chopped

Cook bacon in large skillet over medium-high for 10 to 12 minutes, until just done. Transfer to paper towels to drain.

Place flour in bowl and add the seasonings I have here or your favourite seasonings. Dredge steaks in seasoned flour, place in skillet and cook over high for 8 to 12 minutes, turning occasionally, until almost done. Add mushrooms, onion and bacon. Cook for about 10 more minutes. Serve steaks topped with bacon mixture.

Wild Goose Liver Pâté

Serves 4

As a child growing up La Belle Province, goose liver pâté (or *pâté de foie gras*, as we called it back home) was considered a staple appetizer enjoyed by nearly every family I knew. And it wasn't just those of francophone descent who liked eating foie gras; the English-speaking community also loved it. My parents served it regularly as an appetizer option in their hotel kitchen, and whenever we had guests over, pâté was always available on the coffee table next to a pile of crackers. It is one snack I still enjoy today, and it takes me back to my roots every time.

> 4 oz (113 g) goose liver
> 3/4 cup (175 mL) water
> 1 small onion, thinly sliced, divided
>
> 3 Tbsp (45 mL) butter, softened
> 2 tsp (10 mL) dry sherry
> 1/2 tsp (2 mL) salt
> 1/4 tsp (1 mL) pepper
> 1/4 tsp (1 mL) ground mace

Combine liver, water and all but 2 to 3 slices of onion in medium saucepan. Bring to a boil, reduce heat, cover and simmer for 15 minutes, until liver is cooked. Remove from heat and drain. Discard onion and any large, tough portions of liver.

Dice reserved onion slices. Place liver, onion, butter, sherry, salt, pepper and mace in blender and process until smooth. Remove mixture from blender and form into mound on serving platter. Refrigerate pate for 1 to 2 hours before serving. Serve with crackers as an appetizer.

Stuffed Roasted Goose

Serves 6 to 8

Always use extra caution throughout the entire cooking process when preparing this "king of the waterfowl." Goose can be some of the best fowl you have ever had, but it can also turn out as tough as a board, depending on the recipe and on your level of culinary skill. Using this stuffed roast goose recipe, you will find the bird is usually tender, juicy and just the way you would hope a good roast would turn out.

1 cup (250 mL) water
1/2 cup (125 mL) dry red wine
1 Tbsp (15 mL) molasses
1 tsp (5 mL) pickling spice
2 apples, peeled, cored and diced
1 cup (250 mL) diced dried apricots
1/2 cup (125 mL) raisins

1 Canada goose, cleaned and plucked
1/2 cup (125 mL) lemon juice
1/2 tsp (5 mL) salt
1/2 tsp (5 mL) pepper
1/2 cup (125 mL) bread crumbs
4 oz (113 g) salt pork, thinly sliced

The night before you plan to have the goose for dinner, combine water, wine, molasses and pickling spice in small saucepan over medium heat. Mix well and bring to a simmer. Continue to simmer for about 10 minutes. Add apples, apricots and raisins. Cover and simmer for an additional 5 minutes. Allow to cool, then refrigerate overnight.

Preheat oven to 350°F (175°C). Rub lemon juice on inside and outside of goose, and sprinkle with salt and pepper. Strain stuffing, reserving liquid for later. Stir bread crumbs into stuffing mixture and stuff goose. Place salt pork over goose breast and place goose, breast up, in roasting pan. Cook for approximately 2 hours, basting occasionally with liquid reserved from stuffing. Let stand for 5 minutes before serving.

Roasted Wild Goose

Serves 6 to 8

Many folks use the twice-annual Canada goose migration as a seasonal gauge. Geese flocks migrating in fall usually signal the onset of winter, and geese seen flying overhead in spring signal the arrival of warmer weather. The goose population ranges from stable to increasing in many areas, so it is not uncommon to see fields and flooded marshlands called "staging areas" covered in geese during the spring and fall migrations. As one can imagine, during such a long migration, a tired goose would need a few rest stops along the way.

> salt, sprinkle
> pepper, sprinkle
> cinnamon, sprinkle
> 1 Canada goose, cleaned and plucked
> 3/4 cup (175 mL) red wine vinegar
> 3/4 cup (175 mL) dry sherry
> 1/2 cup (125 mL) peanut oil

Preheat oven to 450°F (230°C). Place goose, breast down, in roasting pan. Sprinkle salt, pepper and cinnamon over entire goose, rubbing spices into skin. Combine vinegar, sherry and oil, and pour over goose. Cook, covered, for 40 minutes. Remove cover and increase oven to broil. Broil 8 minutes. Turn goose breast side up and broil 8 more minutes.

Try with This  **Wild Rice Stuffing**

Makes 4 cups (1 L)

1 cup (250 mL) wild rice
1/4 cup (60 mL) butter
1/2 lb (225 g) fresh mushrooms, sliced
2 1/2 tsp (12 mL) diced onion
1/4 tsp (1 mL) ground sage
1/4 tsp (1 mL) ground thyme
salt and pepper

Cook rice according to package directions. Melt butter in skillet over medium, and sauté mushrooms and onion until lightly browned. Add cooked wild rice and herbs; mix well. Add salt and pepper to taste. This recipe goes well with all game birds.

Goose on the Rotisserie

Serves 6 to 8

According to avid conservationist and wild game aficionado Grant Bailey, you should always be careful of singeing when cooking wild geese. The small pin feathers often remain intact on a freshly plucked goose. The smell and taste of burnt feathers will linger a long time and affect the final product, even if rinsed and frozen. Bailey says you could go to the effort of stripping these small feathers with hot wax, but that is quite labour intensive. The easiest option is just to leave the few remaining feathers in place and avoid eating the skin altogether.

> 1/2 cup (125 mL) butter, softened
> 2 tsp (10 mL) anchovy paste
> 1/4 tsp (1 mL) lemon juice
> 1/4 tsp 1 mL) hot pepper sauce
> 1 Canada goose, cleaned and plucked

Mix first 4 ingredients together. Rub butter mixture on goose and reserve leftovers for basting. Place goose on rotisserie and cook for 1 1/2 hours over medium heat, basting with anchovy butter as often as possible. Let stand for 5 minutes before serving.

Try with This  **Garlic Couscous**

Serves 4

1 Tbsp (15 mL) extra-virgin olive oil
1 garlic clove, minced
1 cup (250 mL) couscous
1 cup (250 mL) prepared chicken broth
1/3 cup (75 mL) grated Parmesan cheese
1/4 tsp (1 mL) salt
1/4 tsp (1 mL) pepper

In medium saucepan over medium-high, combine oil and garlic and heat until oil bubbles slightly. Pour in couscous and chicken broth, and bring to a boil. Simmer on low for 5 to 7 minutes, until liquid is absorbed by couscous. Add cheese, salt and pepper, and serve.

Grilled Canada Goose

Serves 6 to 8

It has been said that there is no good recipe for wild goose because the flesh is usually tough. Some recipes even specify "young goose" in an effort to mitigate the situation. Moist cooking methods allow for the eventual softening of the meat. Some experienced chefs, like Grant Bailey, cover the goose with bacon slices or cheesecloth dipped in melted butter to keep it from drying out. The breast meat is best described as dense, with the legs being even denser. However, when prepared properly, goose can be a great-tasting meal.

1 Canada goose, cleaned and plucked
1/4 cup (60 mL) extra-virgin olive oil
1 tsp (5 mL) garlic powder
1 tsp (5 mL) onion powder
1/2 tsp (2 mL) salt
1/2 tsp (2 mL) pepper

Preheat grill to medium, and spray with nonstick cooking spray. Cut goose in half down breastbone and coat both halves completely with olive oil. Season both goose halves with garlic powder, onion powder, salt and pepper. Place goose halves on grill, skin side up. Cook for 15 to 20 minutes, flipping to skin side down halfway through. Goose is done when meat is no longer pink and pulls away easily from breastbone. Remove from grill and let stand for 5 minutes before carving.

 CLEANING AND PLUCKING GOOSE

Pull out all the feathers by hand and discard them. Don't worry about removing the tiny pin feathers—they will quickly singe off and burn on the grill. Tear back the skin on the underside of the bird at the stomach cavity. Remove and discard the entrails, then rinse the goose under cool water and pat dry with paper towel.

Orange Goose Breasts

Serves 8

Canada geese are very common, but there are several other species of goose in Canada. The snow goose is a less common and slightly smaller goose occasionally seen during its spring or fall migration. The snow goose is a beautiful bird, usually mostly white, but some, known as "blue geese," are darker. The snow goose shares similar habitat and migration patterns with the Canada goose, though it spends its summers much farther north. The geese are similar in taste, although the snow goose is less commonly used for cooking purposes, being less common period.

4 goose breasts, halved
1/2 tsp (2 mL) salt
1/2 tsp (2 mL) pepper

1 garlic clove, minced
1 Tbsp (15 mL) soy sauce
1 Tbsp (15 mL) grated orange zest
juice of 1 orange
1 tsp (5 mL) lemon juice
1 tsp (5 mL) brown sugar
1/2 tsp (2 mL) dry mustard

Preheat oven to 350°F (175°C). Place breasts in baking dish. Season with salt and pepper.

In bowl, mix together garlic, soy sauce, orange zest, orange juice, lemon juice and brown sugar. Add mustard and mix. Pour mixture over breasts in baking dish and cook, basting occasionally, for about 30 minutes, until tender and juices run clear. Let stand for 5 minutes before serving.

Fried Goose

Serves 2

If you live in Canada, you have likely heard the characteristic "honk" of a Canada goose, but did you know that geese actually communicate with a variety of different calls? From the time they are goslings still in the egg, geese use a wide range of sounds to communicate with one another. Scientific research has actually uncovered more than a dozen distinct calls or sounds used by geese to communicate such things as joy, warnings or various types of greeting. Next time you hear the honk of a Canada goose, you can be sure that it is saying something to the rest of the flock.

1 goose breast, halved
1 cup (250 mL) soy sauce
1 cup (250 mL) flour
1/2 tsp (2 mL) onion powder
1/2 tsp (2 mL) garlic powder
1/2 tsp (2 mL) pepper
1/2 cup (125 mL) canola oil

Tenderize meat with meat tenderizer or mallet. Place soy sauce in bowl. In another bowl, combine flour, onion powder, garlic powder and pepper. Dip meat in soy sauce, then roll in flour mixture. Heat oil in cast-iron skillet over medium. Add meat and cook for about 7 minutes per side, until browned. Transfer to paper towel to drain.

 MEAT TENDERIZERS

Tenderizing meat with a commercial meat tenderizer or meat mallet is a simple way to improve the texture of an otherwise tough piece of meat. Most mallets on the market are wood or metal and have one smooth side and one bumpy side. The raised points on the bumpy side are called "tenderizers" and break down fibre when struck against meat. Typically you use the tenderizer side of the mallet on both sides of the meat. A tenderizer can work wonders on a tough meat such as goose.

Slow Cooker Goose

Serves 6

The Canada goose is a symbol of nature and all things wild in our great country. It is perhaps the most adaptable and wide-ranging waterfowl species in all of North America. In central Canada, in particular, the Canada goose has evolved into its own distinct sub-species, a bird that has abandoned the inborn need to migrate. These oversized Canada geese are known as "giant Canadas" and are wreaking havoc in parks across much of central Canada and the West. Managing these geese is very tricky, as they are causing substantial damage in parks and are outcompeting other winter species that would normally be using the habitat.

> 1/2 cup (125 mL) soy sauce
> 4 tsp (20 mL) canola oil
> 4 tsp (20 mL) lemon juice
> 2 tsp (10 mL) Worcestershire sauce
> 1 tsp (5 mL) garlic powder
> 2 lbs (900 g) goose breast, cut into
>   1-inch (2.5 cm) cubes
>
> 3/4 cup (175 mL) flour
> 1/4 cup (60 mL) butter, cubed
>
> 1 x 10 oz (284 mL) can condensed cream
>   of mushroom soup
> 1 1/3 cups (325 mL) water
> 1 envelope onion soup mix

In bowl, mix together soy sauce, oil, lemon juice, Worcestershire sauce and garlic powder. Add goose meat. Stir to coat, then cover and refrigerate for minimum of 4 hours.

Remove meat from marinade. Dredge meat in flour to coat. Melt butter in large skillet over medium, add meat and cook until browned.

Transfer browned meat to slow cooker. Mix together mushroom soup, water and onion soup mix, and add mixture to slow cooker. Cook on Low for 7 to 8 hours, until meat is tender.

Canada Goose Stew

Serves 4

You may have noticed that this book features many stew recipes. It is partly because I am a huge fan of stews but also because I believe that wild game stew, regardless of the game meat featured in it, is a traditionally Canadian dish. There are so many varieties and variations, including this Canada goose stew recipe. Creating stew is a labour of love every time. I have yet to find someone who is not a fan of stew, and I am forever learning new ways to recreate this great Canadian staple.

> **2 goose breasts, halved**
> **1 red onion, chopped**
> **1 red pepper, chopped**
> **2 green peppers, chopped**
> **2 carrots, chopped**
> **2 garlic cloves, minced**
> **1 x 28 oz (796 mL) can diced tomatoes**
> **1 cup (250 mL) sliced mushrooms**
> **1/2 tsp (2 mL) salt**
> **1/2 tsp (2 mL) pepper**

Cut goose into bite-sized stew pieces and place in slow cooker. Add remaining ingredients, stir, and cook on Low for 7 to 8 hours.

Try with This  **Artichokes with Lemon Garlic Butter**

Serves 4

4 fresh artichokes
1/4 cup (60 ml) olive oil
2 garlic cloves, minced
1/4 cup (60 mL) lemon juice
1/2 cup (125 mL) butter
1/4 tsp (1 mL) salt
1/4 tsp (1 mL) pepper

Prepare artichokes by cutting stems and top 1 1/2 inches (4 cm) off. Cut away first outside row of leaves and tips. Steam artichokes in vegetable steamer for about 30 minutes, until tender.

Meanwhile, heat oil in small pot over medium. Add garlic; cook for 1 minute. Add lemon juice, butter, salt and pepper; whisk until butter melts. Serve artichokes warm with seasoned butter.

Goose Burgers

Serves 4

Geese have been given a bad culinary rap. Although they can be a bit fatty and somewhat strong in taste, this goose burger recipe will serve as a great alternative to the traditional beef hamburger we all know. It is a fabulous way to enjoy goose without having to worry about whether it is tough or having to be concerned about an overly strong or greasy flavour. Goose burgers, simply put, are delicious.

1 lb (454 g) ground goose breast
1/3 cup (75 mL) Italian dressing
1/2 tsp (2 mL) pepper, divided

1 cup (250 mL) flour
1/2 tsp (2 mL) salt
1/4 tsp (1 mL) garlic powder

3 Tbsp (45 mL) vegetable oil
4 hamburger buns

In large bowl, mix together ground goose, Italian dressing and 1/4 tsp (1 mL) pepper. Refrigerate for minimum 1 hour.

In small bowl, mix together flour, salt, remaining 1/4 tsp (1 mL) pepper and garlic powder. Spread out flour mixture on sheet of wax paper. Form goose mixture into 4 equal sized balls. Flatten 1 ball into patty on flour mixture. Flip over and coat other side. Repeat for other 3 balls.

Heat oil in skillet over medium. Fry patties for about 10 minutes, flipping once or twice, until well cooked. Serve on hamburger buns; add whatever toppings you prefer.

Pictured on page 123.

Goose Burgers (p. 122), Old-style Onion Rings (p. 161)

Duck Teriyaki Appetizer (p. 125), Bison Bites (p. 77)

Duck Teriyaki Appetizer

Serves 10

The mallard and the black duck are two of Canada's most popular waterfowl, both from a commercial standpoint and from a sporting aspect. The mallard duck is quite distinctive and wide ranging. The male sports an emerald green head and can be found on many small ponds and marshlands. Mallard and black ducks share similar habitat and, except for some markings and a bit of colour variation, are also similar in appearance. Black ducks and mallards also produce a hybrid of the two species. Differentiating between the hybrid species and a purebred mallard or black is very difficult. Biologists and hunters use a patch on the duck's wings known as a speculum to differentiate the species.

1/2 cup (125 mL) teriyaki sauce
1 Tbsp (15 mL) soy sauce
1 Tbsp (15 mL) peanut oil
1 tsp (5 mL) minced ginger root
2 boneless duck breast halves, cut into 1-inch (2.5 cm) cubes

10 slices bacon, cut in half
20 small chunks pineapple

In small bowl, mix together teriyaki sauce, soy sauce, peanut oil and ginger. Add duck meat and marinate for minimum 1 hour.

Preheat oven to 500°F (260°C). Remove meat from marinade and wrap each piece with 1 chunk of pineapple in 1 piece of bacon. Use wooden toothpicks to hold bacon together. Place on baking sheet and cook for about 10 minutes, until bacon is crisp.

Pictured on page 124.

Marinated Roast Duck

Serves 4

The waterfowl population in Canada, including the various duck species, is a work in progress. The most important aspect to managing waterfowl involves habitat management. Groups such as Ducks Unlimited Canada spend millions of dollars each year working with biologists, hunters and conservationists with the ultimate goal of managing waterfowl habitat on a sustained yield basis. Thanks to the efforts of Ducks Unlimited, most species of ducks and geese in this country have stable populations and are kept under a close watchful eye.

4 garlic cloves, minced
1/4 cup (60 mL) honey
1/4 cup (60 mL) soy sauce
2 Tbsp (30 mL) orange juice
2 Tbsp (30 mL) minced ginger root
1 Tbsp (15 mL) sugar
3/4 tsp (4 mL) salt
3/4 tsp (4 mL) pepper
1 x 2 to 3 lb (900 g to 1.4 kg) duck, rinsed and patted dry

1/4 cup (60 mL) sliced green onion

In large bowl, mix together first 8 ingredients. Place duck in marinade, turn to coat, cover bowl and refrigerate overnight.

Preheat oven to 350°F (175°C). Place duck breast up in roasting pan and stuff with green onion. Place in oven and cook for about 2 hours, until juices run clear, basting occasionally. Let stand for 5 minutes before serving.

Try with This  **Cold Rice Salad**

Serves 4 to 6

2 cups (500 mL) cooked rice
1 cup (250 mL) frozen peas, thawed
1/4 cup (60 mL) chopped green pepper
1/4 cup (60 mL) chopped celery
1 Tbsp (15 mL) diced green onion
1 Tbsp (15 mL) vegetable oil
1/2 tsp (2 mL) salt
1/2 tsp (2 mL) pepper
1/4 tsp (1 mL) ground nutmeg

Combine first 5 ingredients in large bowl. Whisk together remaining ingredients and stir into rice mixture. Cover and refrigerate for 2 hours before serving.

Duck

Saucy Roast Duck

Serves 4

Most Canadian puddle ducks are ground and cover nesters, which is to say they lay their eggs adjacent to marshlands, usually on the ground and protected by some cover. Other ducks are cavity nesters. The beautifully coloured wood duck is the most famous cavity nester that we have in Canada. A cavity nester will build a nest in a cavity carved out of a tree. Because wood ducks are not equipped with the bill of a woodpecker, they often use nests previously built by pileated woodpeckers. On well-managed marshlands, wildlife biologists will construct and strategically locate wood duck nesting boxes. It is all part of waterfowl management.

> 1 small onion, chopped
> 1 garlic clove, minced
> 1 cup (250 mL) butter
> 1/2 cup (125 mL) ketchup
> 1 1/2 Tbsp (22 mL) lemon juice
> 1 Tbsp (15 mL) Worcestershire sauce
> 1/2 tsp (2 mL) hot pepper sauce
> 1/2 tsp (2 mL) salt
> 1/2 tsp (2 mL) pepper
>
> 1 x 2 to 3 lb (900 g to 1.4 kg) duck, rinsed and patted dry

Preheat oven to 350°F (175°C). In small pot, combine all ingredients except duck and heat, stirring, for about 5 minutes, until butter is melted and ingredients blend.

Split ducks in half lengthwise, and place duck halves in roasting pan breast up, and pour sauce over top. Cook for approximately 2 hours, until juices run clear (no blood), basting every 15 minutes or so. Let stand for 5 minutes before serving.

Sweet and Sour Duck

Serves 6 to 8

A few aspects must be considered when cooking duck. Although it is poultry like chicken or like grouse and pheasant in the wild game category, duck is more a red meat than most poultry and, as a result, will retain a slightly pinkish centre when cooked, more like beef steak. Chefs generally aim to achieve an internal temperature of 160°F (70°C) for properly cooked duck. And, as with other wild meats and poultries, it is a good idea to let the meat rest following cooking to allow the juices to settle in the meat.

2 x 2 to 3 lb (900 g to 1.4 kg) ducks, rinsed and patted dry
1 orange, sliced
1 apple, sliced
2 Tbsp (30 mL) vegetable oil

3/4 cup (175 mL) ketchup
1/4 cup (60 mL) white vinegar
1/4 cup (60 mL) Worcestershire sauce
2 Tbsp (30 mL) lemon juice
2 Tbsp (30 mL) brown sugar

Preheat oven to 325°F (160°C). Stuff duck cavities with orange and apple slices. Rub ducks with oil and place in roasting pan breast up.

Combine remaining ingredients in bowl and mix well; spoon over ducks. Cover with foil and cook for 2 hours. Remove foil and continue to cook for another 30 minutes, until browned and internal temperature is 160°F (70°C). Let stand for 5 minutes before serving.

Orange Duck

Serves 4

The common duck is divided into two categories: the puddle duck and the diving duck. Diving ducks tend to spend much of their lives on large bodies of water. They are built so that they may dive to great depths to retrieve aquatic plants and insects, molluscs and crustaceans. Common diving ducks include the ring-necked duck and lesser scaup. The most common duck from both a culinary and sporting aspect is the puddle duck. Common puddle ducks in Canada are the mallard, black duck, wood duck, blue-winged teal and green-winged teal.

1 x 2 to 3 lb (900 g to 1.4 kg) duck, rinsed and patted dry
1 orange, sliced

3/4 cup (175 mL) frozen concentrated orange juice, thawed
2 Tbsp (30 mL) orange marmalade
1 envelope poultry gravy mix
1/4 cup (60 mL) flour
2 Tbsp (30 mL) brown sugar
1/2 tsp (2 mL) garlic powder
1/2 tsp (2 mL) salt

Preheat oven to 350°F (175°C). Place duck breast up in roasting pan. Open duck cavity and stuff with orange slices.

Combine remaining ingredients in bowl and mix well. Pour mixture over duck. Cook for approximately 2 hours, until juices run clear, basting every 15 minutes or so. Let stand for 5 minutes before serving.

Asian Grilled Mallard

Serves 2

When cooking duck for the first time, be it wild or the domestic variety, you should know a few things. Duck is a somewhat fatty meat with a thick layer of skin, which becomes quite crispy when grilled or broiled. Compared to upland game birds, duck breasts contain a lot of natural oils that will cook off in the first few minutes. Some chefs actually drain off the grease in the early stages of cooking. One way to limit the amount of fat in your duck is to remove the skin altogether. Or you could make small slices into the breast meat approximately 1 inch (2.5 cm) apart to allow the grease drain out, thereby improving the overall taste of your bird.

> 1/4 cup (60 mL) soy sauce
> 2 Tbsp (30 mL) extra-virgin olive oil
> 1/2 tsp (2 mL) Sriracha (hot Asian chili sauce)
> 2 Tbsp (30 mL) minced garlic
> 1/4 tsp (1 mL) pepper
>
> 2 duck breasts, halved

In large mixing bowl, combine all ingredients except duck. Add duck breasts and stir to coat. Cover and refrigerate for 2 hours.

Preheat grill to medium-high. Remove duck breasts from marinade and grill for 5 to 10 minutes, flipping at least once, until no longer pink inside. Let stand for 5 minutes before serving.

Pictured on page 141.

Try with This  ## Lemon Brussels Sprouts
Serves 8

4 cups (1 L) Brussels sprouts, trimmed and halved
2 Tbsp (30 mL) butter, softened
1 tsp (5 mL) grated lemon zest
2 tsp (10 mL) lemon juice
salt, sprinkle
pepper, sprinkle

In large pot, boil Brussels sprouts for about 6 minutes, until tender-crisp. Drain and return to pot. Add remaining ingredients; toss and heat until butter melts.

Slow Cooker Duck

Serves 4

Duck is often considered difficult to cook. By using this recipe, the days of struggling with how to prepare duck are over. When cooked in this fashion, the meat is tender and never greasy, and as with most slow cooker dishes, it is not extremely labour intensive. Slow Cooker Duck is the perfect recipe for a weekend at the cottage when you have the time in the morning to prepare the ingredients and then just add them to the pot. Come supper time, a delicious meal will be waiting for you.

> 1 x 2 to 3 lb (900 g to 1.4 kg) duck, rinsed and patted dry
> 1 Tbsp (15 mL) extra-virgin olive oil
> 1 Tbsp (15 mL) poultry seasoning
> salt and pepper
>
> 3 cups (750 mL) prepared chicken broth

Brush thin coat of olive oil on outside of duck and season inside and out with poultry seasoning, and salt and pepper to taste.

Place duck in slow cooker and cook on High for 1 hour. Reduce heat to Low and add broth. Cook for an additional 8 hours, until meat is tender.

Try with This  **Rice with Bacon**

Serves 4

8 slices bacon
1 small onion, diced
1 celery rib, diced
1 carrot, diced
1 green pepper, diced
1/4 cup (60 mL) butter
3 cups (750 mL) cooked white rice

In skillet over medium-high, fry bacon until cooked but not crispy. Remove from skillet and cut into 1/2-inch (12 mm) pieces.

Sauté vegetables in butter over medium for 3 to 4 minutes, until soft. Stir in rice and bacon. Serve warm.

Roasted Ruffed Grouse

Serves 4

Of all the wild game featured in this book, the grouse certainly brings to mind the most memories from my childhood. Grouse were the first game animal I pursued as a young hunter. My pal, Mark McMahon, and I would walk the trails and around the hawthorn bushes behind his farm and near the old dump in Arundel. I can still remember Mark telling me that we should focus on the new hawthorn growth because he had heard those berries would make the grouse drunk when they ate them. The theory was that a drunken grouse might fly a bit slower and give us young lads a fighting chance when it came to hunting. Whatever the case, we spent many hours walking those trails looking for hawthorn bushes and we did harvest the odd bird, but I don't believe the berries slowed them down much.

> 4 grouse breasts, rinsed and patted dry
> 1 tsp (5 mL) garlic powder
> 1 tsp (5 mL) pepper
> 1 lemon, sliced
> 1/3 cup (75 mL) butter, melted
> 4 slices bacon, halved
> 3 celery ribs, chopped
> 1 onion, chopped
> 1 x 10 oz (284 mL) can sliced mushrooms, drained
> 1 Tbsp (15 mL) chicken bouillon powder

Preheat oven to 350°F (175°C). Sprinkle grouse breasts with garlic powder and pepper. Place breasts in roasting pan and arrange lemon slices around them. Dribble butter over breasts and drape bacon slices on top of each one. Mix together celery, onion, mushrooms and bouillon powder and add mixture to bottom of roasting pan. Cook for about 1 1/2 hours, or until breasts are cooked through and tender. Let stand for 5 minutes before serving.

Ruffed Grouse with Mint

Serves 4

The grouse family includes such species as the ruffed grouse, the spruce grouse, the sage grouse and the sharp-tailed grouse. They are one of the most popular upland game birds, from a sporting aspect, and reside in Canada in substantial numbers. Anyone who has walked a backwoods trail in southern and central Canada may have been startled by the sound of a flushing grouse. These birds typically feed on the forest floor, although they do fly and can be found occasional evenings roosting in the limbs and boughs of softwood trees.
The "drumming" of the male grouse in spring is distinctive and memorable.

4 grouse breasts, rinsed and patted dry
4 slices bacon, chopped

4 hard-boiled eggs, peeled and diced
1 egg, slightly beaten
2 Tbsp (30 mL) lemon juice
2 Tbsp (30 mL) chopped fresh mint
1/4 tsp (1 mL) ground ginger
1/2 tsp (2 mL) salt
1/2 tsp (2 mL) pepper

1/4 cup (60 mL) prepared chicken broth
1/4 cup (60 mL) butter, melted

Preheat oven to 350°F (175°C). Place breasts in baking dish and scatter bacon over top.

In bowl, mix together hard-boiled eggs, beaten egg, lemon juice, mint, ginger, salt and pepper. Spread egg mixture over breasts.

In small bowl, combine broth and butter. Pour mixture over breasts. Place cover on dish and cook for approximately 40 minutes, until breasts are no longer pink. Baste with pan juices every 15 minutes or so. Let stand for 5 minutes before serving.

Roast Grouse

Serves 2

The grouse will forever remind me of my old hunting companion, Ken Campbell. I have both hunting and cooking memories with Ken when it comes to grouse, or partridge, as it is often mistakenly called. As teenagers, we would walk the backwoods trails around Lakeview and Arundel, Québec, in search of the wily bird. On occasion, we would get lucky and bag one or two of these plump wild fowls, and Ken would share his culinary skills with me. The man knew his way around a bird, and every recipe cooked using grouse was delectable.

> 2 x 1 lb (454 g) grouse, rinsed and patted dry
> 1 Tbsp (15 mL) lemon juice
> 4 slices bacon
> 1/2 cup (125 mL) red currant jelly

Preheat oven to 350°F (175°C). Rub grouse with lemon juice. Push legs toward breast, and secure with skewer pushed through middle of bird. Cover grouse with bacon slices and place in roasting pan breast up. Cook, uncovered, for about 1 1/2 hours, until tender. Let stand for 5 minutes before serving. Serve with red currant jelly.

Country Baked Grouse in Foil

Serves 4

You will notice that in most grouse recipes, there are provisions to prevent drying. Because grouse is such a lean meat with such a pleasant and mild taste, we must do all we can to retain the moisture and prevent drying. Chefs often drape the bird with bacon or orange slices and, as in this case, wrap it in foil, which also helps retain the natural juices. Whatever technique you use in preparing wild game, always be conscious of the cooking time and temperature; you're looking to achieve a fine balance with these delicate meats. Overcooking can be an appetite killer.

> 4 grouse breasts, rinsed and patted dry
> 1/2 cup (125 mL) melted butter
> 4 slices bacon, each cut into 4 pieces
> 2 Tbsp (30 mL) poultry seasoning
>
> 1/2 cup (125 mL) dry white wine

(continued on next page)

Preheat oven to 350°F (175°C). Brush entire surface of breasts with butter. Drape breasts with bacon slices and sprinkle with poultry seasoning. Place breasts on sheet of heavy duty foil. Bring edges together and seal tightly. Place packet in shallow roasting pan and cook for 45 minutes. Open foil carefully and allow grouse to brown for another 10 minutes.

Remove grouse and set aside. Carefully tip drippings from foil into pan, then use foil to tent grouse breasts to keep them warm. Add wine to drippings, and heat to boiling, stirring. Serve sauce over grouse.

Sautéed Grouse Breasts

Serves 4

When it comes to wild fowl, there are no birds that compare to the coveted ruffed grouse. Because most usable grouse meat is really only the delectable white breast meat, there is usually no reason to retain other parts of this bird for cooking. Most grouse recipes call for breast meat. It may sound like a cliché, but grouse is very close to chicken, and when cooked properly, in a recipe that adds a bit of moisture, I think they taste better than chicken.

1/2 cup (125 mL) flour
1/2 tsp (2 mL) garlic powder
1/4 tsp (1 mL) paprika
1/4 tsp 1 mL) crushed dried rosemary
1/2 tsp (2 mL) salt
1/2 tsp (2 mL) pepper
4 boneless grouse breasts, cut into
    1-inch (2.5 cm) cubes

1/3 cup (75 mL) extra-virgin olive oil
3 Tbsp (45 mL) butter
2 garlic cloves, minced

In bowl, combine flour, garlic powder, paprika, rosemary, salt and pepper. Dredge meat in flour mixture.

In large skillet, heat olive oil, butter and garlic over medium and add partridge. Cook for 5 to 7 minutes, until golden brown. Let stand for 5 minutes before serving.

Grouse on the Grill

Serves 4

The ruffed grouse is, in my opinion, the king of all upland game birds. Found throughout the provinces in areas south of the Canadian Shield, the spunky and plump little birds are a challenge in the field and a joy to behold on the table. Most grouse recipes include bacon or bacon drippings; this "secret element" offers the fat-free and somewhat dry flesh of the grouse a bit of moisture. If you have never tried grilled wild grouse, do yourself a favour and give it a shot.

1/2 garlic clove, minced
1/2 onion, diced
3 Tbsp (45 mL) pomegranate molasses
1 tsp (5 mL) lime juice
1 tsp (5 mL) ground cinnamon
1 tsp (5 mL) ground cumin

4 grouse breasts, rinsed and patted dry
salt, sprinkle
pepper, sprinkle

1 cup (250 mL) diced bacon
1/2 garlic clove, minced
1/4 cup (60 mL) pomegranate molasses
1/2 cup (125 mL) whole pistachios

Combine first 6 ingredients in bowl to make marinade.

Season birds with salt and pepper and place in marinade. Cover and refrigerate for 3 to 4 hours.

(continued on next page)

 POMEGRANATE MOLASSES

Pomegranate molasses can also be found under the name pomegranate syrup. It is made by reducing the sweet juice of the pomegranate fruit down to a syrupy liquid and looks very much like traditional molasses. In the Middle East, pomegranate molasses is used in a variety of dishes, most notably in rice pilaf. Here in Canada, you will find this ingredient sold in most Middle Eastern or Turkish markets.

Preheat grill to medium. Fry bacon in pan until crispy. Drain off all but 1 Tbsp (15 mL) of bacon grease. Add remaining ingredients and heat to make a sauce. Remove grouse from marinade and place on grill. Cook for 15 to 20 minutes, turning often, until no longer pink and meat separates easily from breast bone. Serve with sauce.

Partridge Stew

Serves 4

It's amazing how the ruffed grouse has learned to live in a suburban setting and adapt to its ever-changing environment. One "partridge," who we called Lori after the character in the hit 1970s television show, was about as tame as any wild animal I had ever seen. My daughters were young at the time, probably three or four years old. They would be playing in the backyard, and Lori would go strutting by in all her glory, without hesitation. Between strolling around our back lawn in the afternoons and roosting on the edge of our gazebo in the evenings, she would often walk right up to the girls and tilt her head sideways as if to say, "Hey, what are you doing here?" It just goes to show how we can live in harmony with nature.

4 grouse breasts, rinsed and patted dry
6 cups (1.5 L) water, divided
2 cups (500 mL) chopped onions, divided

2 cups (500 mL) chopped carrots
1 1/2 cups (375 mL) rice
salt and pepper

Place grouse breasts, 4 cups (1 l) water and 1 cup (250 mL) onion in saucepan. Bring to a boil, then reduce heat and simmer for 2 hours.

Remove grouse from pot (leave broth). Remove meat from bones and chop into small pieces, then add back to pot. Add carrots, remaining 1 cup (250 mL) onion, remaining 2 cups (500 mL) water and rice. Cover and simmer for about 20 minutes, until carrots are tender and rice is cooked. Add salt and pepper to taste, stir and serve.

Creamed Grouse

Serves 4

The ruffed grouse exhibits some behavioural and physiological differences depending on where it is found. The brown and grey are the two colour phases commonly found in this species. Grouse living in southern Canada tend to be more the brown phase, while those grouse in the north are more commonly seen in the grey phase. Also, the grouse in southern Canada, in areas of high human populations, have evolved into a more skittish and wary creature. In the north, however, grouse tend to fly less and walk more, and they are not as wary of man—welcome news for upland game hunters.

> 4 grouse breasts, rinsed and patted dry
> 1/2 tsp (2 mL) salt
> 1/2 tsp (2 mL) pepper
> paprika, sprinkle
> 3/4 cup (175 mL) flour
> 1/2 cup (125 mL) butter
>
> 2 Tbsp (30 mL) lemon juice
> 2 cups (500 mL) sliced mushrooms
> 1 medium onion, finely chopped
> 1/2 cup (125 mL) ripe olives, sliced

Preheat oven to 325°F (160°C). Split breasts and sprinkle with salt, pepper and paprika. Coat with flour. Melt butter in skillet and brown breasts. Transfer to roasting pan.

Add remaining ingredients to same skillet, and heat for 5 minutes. Pour mixture over breasts in roasting pan. Cook in oven for 1 hour. Let stand for 5 minutes before serving.

Fried Grouse Tenders

Serves 4

I will never forget the first time I tried Fried Grouse Tenders. It was during a moose hunt back in 1994. Because grouse were always a big part of our moose season, we enjoyed one big meal of them each fall. We always arrived at moose camp a couple of days before the season, allowing time to open up the camp, cut some wood and hunt some grouse before the moose hunt got underway. One particular evening I attempted my first fried grouse meal. I was amazed at how it turned out. This recipe is a simple and tasty way of serving the feistiest bird in the upland forest.

> 3 eggs, beaten
> 1 cup (250 mL) milk
> 2 cups (500 mL) flour
> 1/2 tsp (2 mL) salt
> 1/2 tsp (2 mL) pepper
> 4 grouse breasts, cut into strips
> 2 cups (500 mL) vegetable oil

Place egg and milk in 1 bowl and flour, salt and pepper in another bowl. Dip grouse strips in egg mixture and then dredge in flour mixture to coat generously. Heat oil in deep cast-iron skillet and test temperature with popcorn kernel. Lay grouse strips in skillet and fry for 3 to 5 minutes per side, until golden brown. Transfer to paper towels to drain. Serve hot.

 tip   **COOKING OIL TEMPERATURE**

Cookinq with oil can be a fun and tasty way to prepare several wild game dishes, but finding the right cooking temperature can be difficult if you don't have a deep-fry thermometer. A simple technique called the "corn kernel pop" has served me well over the years. You simply drop one popcorn kernel into your oil when it's heating up. The corn kernel will pop open between 350°F and 375°F (175°C and 190°C), which is the optimal oil temperature for most dishes. Once the kernel has popped, simply take it out and start cooking.

Roast Pheasant

Serves 6 to 8

A somewhat rare bird in this country, the ring-necked pheasant is intriguing, to say the least. It was one of the early introductions to this country from Asia and has taken off since the 1800s, becoming established in most provinces. As with some big game animals, the pheasant is polygamous, where one adult male may breed with several hens. This means that there does not need to be a one to one sex ratio to keep a balanced population—good news because it is the male most often pursued by hunters. The male pheasant weighs anywhere from 2 to 3 pounds (1 to 1.5 kg), making it one of the larger upland game birds in Canada.

1/2 cup (125 mL) butter, softened
1 Tbsp (15 mL) chopped fresh thyme
1 Tbsp (15 mL) chopped fresh parsley
2 pheasants, rinsed and patted dry
1/2 tsp (2 mL) garlic powder
1/2 tsp (2 mL) salt
1/2 tsp (2 mL) pepper
1/4 cup (60 mL) vegetable oil

1/2 cup (125 mL) dry red wine

Preheat oven to 375°F (190°C). In bowl, combine butter with herbs. Lift skin away from pheasants and rub herb butter under skin. Season birds with salt, pepper and garlic powder. Place oil in roasting pan, then add pheasants breast up. Cook in oven for about 45 minutes, basting occasionally.

Remove from oven and pour wine over meat. Return to oven for an additional 15 minutes, or until juices run clear when meat is pierced with a fork. Let stand for 5 minutes before serving.

Asian Grilled Mallard (p. 130)
Easy Vegetable Rice (p.164)

Tasty Venison Meatballs (p. 24)

Orange Pheasant

Serves 4

The ring-necked pheasant is an intriguing animal and not one we see every day in Canada. Although most provinces boast localized populations, pheasant numbers fluctuate. According to the breeding birds survey published by the Canadian Wildlife Service, the only provinces with substantial pheasant populations are British Columbia, Alberta, Saskatchewan, Ontario and Nova Scotia. Of those areas, it appears Nova Scotia has the strongest pheasant growth since the 1970s. Breeding bird numbers in Ontario reached an all-time low in 2006, but have slowly been on the rise ever since.

> 1 pheasant, rinsed and patted dry
> 1/2 tsp (2 mL) poultry seasoning
> 3 Tbsp (45 mL) butter
>
> 1 tsp (5 mL) chicken bouillon powder
> 1 cup (250 mL) water
>
> 1/2 cup (125 mL) orange marmalade
> 1/4 cup (60 mL) orange juice

Skin pheasant and split it in half lengthwise. Sprinkle with poultry seasoning. In large skillet over medium heat, melt butter and cook pheasant on both sides until browned.

In small bowl, mix bouillon powder and water, then pour over pheasant. Cover skillet, reduce heat and simmer for about 30 minutes, until tender.

Drain off any remaining liquid in skillet. Combine marmalade and juice and spoon it over pheasant in skillet. Simmer, uncovered, for 15 minutes, basting often.

Baked Pheasant

Serves 4

Not only is the ring-necked pheasant one of the most beautifully coloured upland game birds in North America, but it is also one of the rarest, so actually seeing one in the wild doesn't happen very often. I have in my lifetime seen but two pheasants. The first one was at my hunt camp more than 20 years ago, when a few of us were doing some repairs and, to our surprise, a hen pheasant walked across the clearing. Then one day about 10 years ago at my home in the Ottawa area, an adult male ring-neck strolled onto our property. I couldn't believe my eyes, and unfortunately, I did not have a camera handy at the time.

1 egg
2 Tbsp (30 mL) milk
1/2 tsp (2 mL) garlic powder
1/2 tsp (2 mL) onion powder
1 cup (250 mL) crushed cornflakes cereal
1/2 cup (125 mL) grated Parmesan cheese

1/4 cup (60 mL) butter

1 pheasant, rinsed, patted dry and cut into pieces
1/2 tsp (2 mL) pepper

Preheat oven to 375°F (190°C). In bowl, combine egg, milk, garlic powder and onion powder. In separate bowl, combine cornflakes and Parmesan cheese.

Melt butter and pour into baking dish or casserole.

Dip pheasant pieces in egg mixture, then roll in cornflakes mixture to coat. Place skin-side down in baking dish. Season with pepper. Bake, uncovered, for about 1 hour, until meat is cooked through. Let stand for 5 minutes before serving.

Pheasant

Slow Cooker Pheasant

Serves 6 to 8

Recipes such as this slow cooker dish are ideal for cooking wild pheasant—as well as other game birds—because they require a slow cook on a low heat to keep them from drying out. The low, simmering heat and the steaming action of a slow cooker is perhaps the best way to produce a moist, tender pheasant meal. These birds do not have a strong gamey taste, and if you are purchasing commercially raised pheasant, the younger specimens are the best choice for a moist, succulent meal.

1/2 cup (125 mL) water
1/4 cup (60 mL) salt
2 pheasants, rinsed, patted dry and cut into pieces

1/3 (75 mL) cup soy sauce
3 Tbsp (45 mL) Worcestershire sauce
3 Tbsp (45 mL) balsamic vinegar
3 Tbsp (45 mL) brown sugar
2 Tbsp (30 mL) minced garlic
1 Tbsp (15 mL) liquid smoke
1 Tbsp (15 mL) hot pepper sauce

1/2 cup (125 mL) water

Combine water and salt in large bowl. Place pheasant pieces in salt water to soak for 1 hour.

In small bowl, mix together remaining ingredients. Remove pheasant from salt water and place in large resealable plastic bag. Pour in marinade, seal bag and refrigerate for minimum 2 hours.

Transfer pheasant pieces to slow cooker and discard marinade. Add water. Cover and simmer on Low for 8 hours.

Creamy Slow Cooker Quail

Serves 6 to 8

The quail species native to Canada is the northern bobwhite, which has a limited range mostly in southern Ontario. It is a small, plump bird, and the male has a distinctive brown-black eye stripe that contrasts its white eyebrow and throat. The female sports less distinctive colours, with a dark brown eye stripe on a paler eyebrow and throat. Northern bobwhites are not as heavily pursued by hunters in Canada as in the United States. There are, however, avid upland game bird hunters in southwestern Ontario who do pursue them. Many bird clubs even train their pointing dogs in areas inhabited by the bobwhite. As you can imagine, their modest size makes them quite challenging for hunters.

1 cup (250 mL) flour
1/2 tsp (2 mL) salt
1/2 tsp (2 mL) pepper
8 quail, cut up

1/2 cup (125 mL) oil

2 x 10 oz (284 mL) cans condensed cream of chicken soup
2 x 10 oz (284 mL) cans condensed cream of celery soup
2 x 10 oz (284 mL) cans condensed chicken broth
1/2 cup (125 mL) dry white wine
2 onions, thinly sliced
2 bay leaves

1/3 cup (75 mL) grated Parmesan cheese

In bowl, combine flour, salt and pepper. Dredge quail pieces in flour mixture.

Heat oil in skillet and add quail. Cook until browned.

Transfer quail to slow cooker and add soups, broth, wine, onion and bay leaves. Cook on High for 4 hours, then reduce heat to Low and cook for an additional 2 hours, until meat is tender.

Remove bay leaves, and add Parmesan cheese before serving.

Quail in a Slow Cooker

Serves 4

The quail is perhaps the tiniest game bird featured in this book, but as the saying goes, "What they lack in size, they more than make up for in taste." Quail is a mild, tasty and very pleasant wild fowl. It is ideal prepared and served in recipes such as this slow cooker one. Always be careful and work slowly when trimming quail meat, because as their petite size sometimes makes them difficult to work with.

4 quail, skinned and deboned
1 onion, chopped
1 cup (250 mL) chopped celery
1 cup (250 mL) baby carrots
2 cups (500 mL) water

1/2 cup (125 mL) butter
1/2 cup (125 mL) flour
2 cups (500 mL) milk
3 Tbsp (45 mL) chicken bouillon powder
1/2 tsp (2 mL) salt
1/2 tsp (2 mL) pepper

Place quail meat in slow cooker. Add onion, celery, carrots and water. Simmer on High for 2 hours.

Melt butter in saucepan over medium, and stir in flour and milk. Add bouillon powder and stir until dissolved. Stir in salt and pepper. Add mixture to slow cooker turn heat to Low and continue simmering for another 4 hours.

Quail Pot Pie

Serves 4

Although the average quail weighs only a little more than 5 oz (140 g), there is actually a fair amount of breast meat. The quail recipes that require meat to be removed will need a bit of work in sizing up the birds and preparing them. In the supermarket, you will often find quail that are dressed and partially prepared. The butcher has a process called "part-boning," where much of the ribcage is removed but the breast meat and legs are left intact. Quail is delicious and well worth the effort in cooking.

1/4 cup (60 mL) butter
1 cup (250 mL) flour
1 tsp (5 mL) baking powder
1/2 tsp (2 mL) dried thyme
1/2 cup (125 mL) half-and-half cream

1/4 cup (60 mL) butter
4 quail, skinned and deboned
1/2 cup (125 mL) sherry

Preheat oven to 350°F (175°C). In bowl, mix together first amount of butter, flour, baking powder and thyme until it forms a crumbly texture. Add cream to flour mixture to form a dough. Place dough on floured board and roll to 1/2-inch (12 mm) thick pastry crust.

In skillet over medium, melt second amount of butter and fry quail meat for about 5 minutes. Remove meat from skillet and place in baking dish. Combine sherry with pan juices and pour over quail in baking dish. Top with crust and pierce with fork in several places. Bake for about 30 minutes, until golden brown.

Grilled Woodies

Serves 8

The American woodcock is migratory: every fall the woodcocks slowly begin to fly south in search of more favourable temperatures. By early spring, the woodcocks, or "timber doodles" as they are sometimes called, have started to return to the woods and meadows of southern Canada. Each May, I am fortunate to be serenaded by the mating ritual of the American woodcock in my back field. To gain the attention of the female, the male woodcock squeaks loudly and then performs spirals high up in the air. It is just one more of the many wonders of nature.

> 8 American woodcock, cleaned and plucked
> 1/2 cup (125 mL) peanut oil
> 1 tsp (5 mL) dried crushed rosemary
> 1 tsp (5 mL) dried thyme
> 1/2 tsp (2 mL) garlic powder
> 1/2 tsp (2 mL) salt
> 1/2 tsp (2 mL) pepper

Preheat grill to medium-high and spray with non-stick cooking spray. Rub each woodcock with peanut oil, making sure to cover it completely. Season each bird with rosemary, thyme, garlic powder, salt and pepper. Place woodcocks on grill and cook for about 10 minutes per side, until meat is no longer pink. Be careful not to overcook.

 ### *tip* CLEANING AND PLUCKING WOODCOCK

The American wookcock is a tiny bird and, as with quail and grouse, the bulk of usable flesh lies in the breast meat. To prepare the woodcock breast for cooking, first remove the wings, legs and head using a sharp kitchen knife or cleaver. Unlike grouse, the woodcock will need to be plucked to expose the breast. Pull the feathers out by hand; don't worry about any small pin feathers remaining, as they will quickly singe and burn off on the grill. Tear back the skin on the underside of the bird. Remove and discard the entrails. Then rinse the breast meat under cool water and pat dry with paper towel.

Asian Woodcock Stir-fry

Serves 4

You will notice that many wild fowl recipes have an Asian-inspired flavour that always involves teriyaki or soy sauce, chosen for the sole purpose of masking the natural game flavours. Game birds turn out wonderfully when cooked under the Asian influence, but be careful, when cooking Asian-style, not to overdo the soy sauce, teriyaki sauce or other salty Asian sauces.

> 2 Tbsp (30 mL) extra-virgin olive oil
> 1 onion, sliced
> 4 woodcock breasts, cut into 1/2-inch (12 mm) slices
> 1 green pepper, sliced
> 1 tomato, cut into chunks
>
> 1 1/2 cups (375 mL) prepared beef broth
> 1/4 cup (60 mL) soy sauce
> 1/4 cup (60 mL) water
> 2 Tbsp (30 mL) flour
> 1/2 tsp (2 mL) pepper

Heat oil in cast-iron skillet over medium-high. Add onions and cook for 5 minutes, until softened. Add woodcock, green pepper and tomato, and cook until meat is lightly browned.

Reduce heat to medium; add broth, soy sauce, water and flour. Season with pepper, then cover and simmer for 5 to 7 minutes, until thickened.

Orange Woodcock

Serves 4

American woodcocks are very small, rarely weighing more than a few ounces, so game bird hunters are very cautious when choosing the shell types they use. Exercise care when skinning, separating the meat from the breast bone, and dressing the woodcock for the table. It is crucial that every last morsel of meat is removed when butterflying or trimming this plump yet tiny bird.

> 1/4 cup (60 mL) butter, melted
> 2 Tbsp (30 mL) orange juice
> 1 tsp (5 mL) lemon juice

(continued on next page)

Woodcock

4 woodcock breasts
1/2 tsp (2 mL) salt
1/2 tsp (2 mL) lemon pepper
2 slices bacon, cut in half
4 orange slices, peeled

Preheat oven to 350°F (175°C). Combine butter, orange juice and lemon juice in small bowl. Keep warm.

Season breasts with salt and lemon pepper. Drape each breast with 1 bacon slice and 1 orange slice. Place breasts in roasting pan and cook for 15 minutes, basting occasionally with butter mixture. Let stand for 5 minutes before serving. Remove cooked bacon and orange slices and serve alongside meat.

Natural Woodcock

Serves 2

Identifying this plump little bird in the wild can be tricky for beginners. Two other birds native to Canada are often mistaken for the American woodcock: the common Wilson's snipe and the spotted sandpiper. They all have a long, needle-like bill, but the woodcock tends to exhibit a plumper or fuller body, with markings more similar to a grouse and with a bill that is slightly shorter than the snipe or the sandpiper. Also, since the woodcock is an upland bird, it is more commonly found in the thick forested and mountainous areas compared to the other two birds, which dwell in more open areas.

1/2 cup (125 mL) flour
1/2 cup (125 mL) salt
3/4 tsp (4 mL) sugar
3/4 tsp (4 mL) garlic powder
2 woodcock breasts

2 Tbsp (30 mL) extra-virgin olive oil
1/4 cup (60 mL) water

Mix together flour, salt, sugar and garlic powder in bowl. Dredge woodcock breasts in flour mixture to coat.

Heat oil in skillet over medium and add breasts. Cook until browned on both sides. Add water. Cover and simmer for 10 minutes, or until tender.

Roasted Wild Turkey

Serves 8 to 10

The wild male turkey can grow to an impressive size and is the target of most gobbler hunting enthusiasts. Mature toms sport what is known as a beard, which is basically a clump of hairs protruding from the birds' lower neck. Some very large toms will occasionally grow two, three and even more beards. Multiple beards are an indication of age, nutrients, habitat and good genetics. Although multi-bearded toms are rare, they do exist and would be considered the dominant male in any wild turkey woods.

> 1 medium onion, chopped
> 2 celery ribs, sliced
> 1 wild turkey, dressed
> 3 Tbsp (45 mL) extra-virgin olive oil

Preheat oven to 350°F (175°C). Place double layer of foil in large roasting pan, leaving enough overlap on each side to close over turkey. Place onion and celery on foil in pan. Brush turkey with oil and place in pan, breast up, on top of onions and celery. Wrap foil around bird, leaving just a small opening at top for steam to escape. Cook in oven for 3 hours. Check thigh for doneness after 2 1/2 hours. Let stand for 10 minutes before carving.

Try with This  ## Game Bird Stuffing

Makes 4 cups (1 L)

4 slices bacon, diced
1/2 cup (125 mL) diced onion
1 garlic clove, minced
1 cup (250 mL) heavy cream
3/4 tsp (4 mL) ground thyme
1/2 tsp (2 mL) ground cinnamon
1/4 tsp (1 mL) celery seed
ground nutmeg, sprinkle
3/4 tsp (4 mL) salt
3/4 tsp (4 mL) pepper
4 cups (1 L) bread cubes
1 egg yolk, lightly beaten
2 Tbsp (30 mL) chopped fresh parsley

In skillet, fry bacon until browned. Add onion and garlic and sauté over medium for 5 minutes. Stir in cream, thyme, cinnamon, celery seed and nutmeg. Simmer for 5 minutes. Stir in salt and pepper.

Pour hot mixture over bread cubes. Add egg yolk and parsley. Stir gently and refrigerate for several hours, until cold and easily clumped. Stuff bird.

152

Honey-glazed Gobbler

Serves 6

Since the pursuit of wild turkey has grown, especially in central Canada, being able to differentiate between a male (tom) and a female (hen) is of utmost importance because the hens are protected from the hunt most of the time to ensure the future of this important game species. It is quite simple to separate the toms from the hens, since the toms are the only gobblers that sport a long beard protruding from their lower neck. The beard may be anywhere from 3 to 4 inches (7.5 to 10 cm) long for a young male to 7 or 8 inches (18 or 20 cm) long on an adult tom. Male gobblers also sport "spurs" near their feet, which are used as a form of protection. The females do not possess these features.

> **vegetable oil for deep frying**
> **2 lbs (900 g) wild turkey breast, cut into strips**
> **1 cup (250 mL) flour**
> **3/4 tsp (4 mL) salt**
> **3/4 tsp (4 mL) pepper**
> **1 egg**
> **3/4 cup (175 mL) milk**
> **1/2 cup (125 mL) liquid honey**

Heat 1/2 inch (12 mm) oil in deep fryer or large skillet to 375°F (190°C). In bowl, combine flour, salt and pepper. Mix egg and milk in separate bowl and stir into flour mixture; stir batter until well mixed. Dip turkey pieces into batter, coating evenly. Put a few pieces at a time in hot oil, and cook for 7 to 10 minutes, until browned. Place on paper towels to drain. Brush turkey strips with honey and serve.

Italian Deep-fried Gobbler

Serves 6

The wild turkey is unique in Canada, not only for its size but also for its vocal abilities. If it were human, it would surely join an *a capella* singing group. The wild turkey is the most vocal of any fowl in this country. As with other species, turkeys use sounds throughout their daily lives. Some more common calls made by the gobbler include the yelp, the cluck, the putt, the keekee, the purr and the gobble. Of course, the most distinctive and most famous wild turkey call is the gobble, a vocalization used mostly by the male, primarily during the spring mating season. Yes, they are one outspoken fowl.

vegetable oil for deep-frying
2 lbs (900 g) wild turkey breast, cut into strips
2 cups (500 mL) Italian dressing
1/2 tsp (2 mL) lemon pepper
2 eggs
2 cups (500 mL) milk
2 cups (500 mL) flour
1/2 tsp (2 mL) salt
1/2 tsp (2 mL) pepper

Preheat oil in deep-fryer to 375°F (190°C). Place turkey strips in large bowl. Add dressing and lemon pepper. In small bowl, beat eggs into milk. In another bowl, mix flour, salt and pepper. Dip turkey strips in egg mixture and then into flour mixture. Deep-fry for 7 to 10 minutes, until golden brown. Transfer to paper towels to drain.

Canadian Wild Turkey Chili

Serves 8

It is astonishing to see how the turkey population in eastern Ontario has exploded over the past few years. I see as many as 30 or even 40 turkeys in nearby fields, and we regularly spot them walking across our property. The gobbler has become a full-time resident here, and it's amazing how we have become used to living with them. Ten and 15 years ago, it was such a novelty to see a gobbler in the wild that to spot one in a field or roosting nearby always generated excitement, whereas today, we see them walking down the road, gathering in the fields and sneaking through the woods. I would say that they are more plentiful in this part of the world than the ruffed grouse.

2 Tbsp (30 mL) vegetable oil
3 lbs (1.4 kg) ground wild turkey breast
1 large onion, diced
2 garlic cloves, minced
1 x 28 oz (796 mL) can diced tomatoes
2 x 14 oz (398 mL) cans tomato sauce
1 Tbsp (15 mL) chili powder
1 tsp (5 mL) salt
1/2 tsp (2 mL) pepper
1/2 tsp (2 mL) cayenne pepper
2 x 14 oz (398 mL) cans pinto beans

Heat oil in large pot over medium-high. Add turkey and cook until browned. Add all remaining ingredients except pinto beans. Cover and simmer for 1 hour. Add beans, and simmer for 1 additional hour.

Wild Turkey Soup

Serves 6

This hearty bird provides terrific table fare given the fact that an adult tom can weigh more than 25 pounds (10 kg). Wild turkey soup, simply put, may be the most delicious soup you will ever have. The times that I have enjoyed wild turkey as a meal, I have found it quite similar to domestic turkey. It is mild and flavourful and, provided it is not overcooked, can be moist as well.

2 Tbsp (30 mL) vegetable oil
1 cup (250 mL) diced onion
1 cup (250 mL) diced celery
1/2 cup (125 mL) diced red pepper
1/4 cup (60 mL) grated carrot
1 lb (454 g) wild turkey breast, cut into 1-inch (2.5 cm) cubes
4 cups (1 L) water
2 Tbsp (30 mL) chicken bouillon powder

1 cup (250 mL) rice
1 large apple, peeled and diced

In large pot, heat oil over medium. Add onion, celery, red pepper and carrot, and cook until tender, 2 or 3 minutes. Add turkey, water and bouillon powder. Increase heat to high, bring to a boil, then reduce heat and simmer for about 15 minutes, until turkey is cooked.

In separate pot, cook rice according to package directions. You can season your rice with whatever you prefer. Add cooked rice and apple cubes to soup and continue to simmer for an additional 5 minutes. Serve with fresh bread or crackers.

Pictured on page 159.

Fried Frog Legs

Serves 2

It is funny how interest in frogs as game meat runs in a cyclical pattern. At one time, frog legs were commonplace on restaurant menus across Canada. Today, you do not see them served as often. Still, some foodies consider frog legs to be a delicacy, and I hope they will make a comeback. When cooked properly and seasoned to perfection, they are every bit as good as domestic chicken. I also hope that recipes such as this one will help bring the tasty frog leg meal back to the forefront.

> 3 Tbsp (45 mL) vegetable oil
> 1/2 tsp (2 mL) diced scallions
> 1 tsp (5 mL) white vinegar
> 1/2 cup (125 mL) flour
> 3/4 tsp (4 mL) salt
> 3/4 tsp (4 mL) pepper
> 6 pairs of frog legs
>
> 3 Tbsp (45 mL) butter

In bowl, combine oil, scallions and vinegar. Combine flour, salt and pepper in separate bowl. Dip each frog leg into oil mixture, then dredge it in flour mixture.

Melt butter in skillet over medium. Place frog legs in skillet and cook until browned. Drain on paper towel.

Québec-style Frog Legs

Serves 6

It is typically the legs of the bullfrog that are harvested for eating because most other frog species in Canada are too small. I recall one Labour Day weekend as a 12-year-old boy with my Uncle Gerry on Beaven Lake, and he brought me frog hunting. I remember thinking, "Surely, he must be joking when he talks about eating frog legs," but sure enough, we did catch a few and serve them at our annual family cookout on the beach. As much a cliché as it is, they do taste like chicken.

3 Tbsp (45 mL) olive oil
1 onion, chopped
2 garlic cloves, minced
2 celery ribs, chopped
1 lb (454 g) tomatoes, peeled, seeded and chopped

1 cup (250 mL) flour
1/2 tsp (2 mL) salt
1/2 tsp (2 mL) pepper
18 pairs of frog legs
1/4 cup (60 mL) butter

Heat oil in skillet over medium, and add onion, garlic and celery. Cook for about 5 minutes. Add tomatoes, stir and cook for 12 to 15 minutes; set aside.

Combine flour, salt and pepper in bowl. Add frog legs and toss to coat. Melt butter in another large skillet over medium. Add frog legs and cook for 5 minutes, until browned. Transfer legs to serving platter and pour tomato mixture over top.

Wild Turkey Soup (p. 156)

Grilled Venison Burgers (p. 25)
and Easy Hamburger Relish (p. 169)

Old-style Onion Rings

Serves 4

canola oil for deep-frying
2 large onions, cut into 1/4-inch (6 mm) slices

1 1/4 cups (300 mL) flour
1 tsp (5 mL) baking powder
1 tsp (5 mL) salt

1 egg
1 cup (250 mL) milk, or as needed

3/4 cup (175 mL) dry bread crumbs

Preheat oil in deep-fryer to 375°F (190°C). Separate onion slices into rings.

In large bowl, combine flour, baking powder and salt. Coat onion rings with flour mixture and then set aside.

Add egg and milk to flour mixture and mix. Dip floured rings into batter to fully coat, and allow excess batter to drip off.

Spread bread crumbs on plate. Run rings through crumbs to coat.

Deep-fry rings, a few at a time, for 2 to 3 minutes, until golden brown. Transfer to paper towels to drain. Serve hot.

Pictured on page 123.

Sautéed Mushrooms

Serves 4

1 Tbsp (15 mL) extra-virgin olive oil
1/2 lb (225 g) fresh mushrooms, sliced
1 tsp (5 mL) dried thyme
1/4 tsp (1 mL) salt

Heat oil in large skillet over medium-high. Once oil is hot, add mushrooms and sauté for 3 or 4 minutes. Add thyme and salt; sauté for an additional 1 to 2 minutes. Serve over any red meat steak or roast.

Stovetop Capellini

Serves 4

8 oz (225 g) capellini pasta

3 Tbsp (45 mL) extra-virgin olive oil
1 garlic clove, minced
1 x 28 oz (796 mL) can diced tomatoes, drained
1 tsp (5 mL) lemon juice
1/8 tsp (0.5 mL) salt
1/8 tsp (0.5 mL) pepper

Cook capellini according to package directions; drain and keep warm.

Heat oil and garlic in large skillet over medium for 5 minutes. Add tomatoes, lemon juice, salt and pepper. Lower heat and simmer for 5 minutes. Add capellini to skillet and stir. Serve hot with any wild game recipe.

Creamy Scalloped Potatoes

Serves 6

1/4 cup (60 mL) butter
1/4 cup (60 mL) flour
1 tsp (5 mL) salt
1/2 tsp (2 mL) pepper
1/2 tsp (2 mL) dried thyme
2 1/2 cups (625 mL) milk

6 large potatoes (about 2 lbs, 900 g), peeled and sliced
1 small onion, sliced

Preheat oven to 350°F (175°C). Melt butter in pot over medium. Add flour, salt, pepper and thyme. Cook, stirring, for 1 minute. Gradually add milk and cook for 5 to 8 minutes, whisking constantly, until boiling and thickened. Set aside.

In baking dish, spread potatoes and onions evenly, and pour sauce over top. Cover and cook for 1 hour. Uncover and cook for about 30 minutes longer, until lightly browned and potatoes are tender. Let stand for 5 minutes before serving to allow sauce to thicken.

Sides

Garlic and Sour Cream Mashed Potatoes

Serves 4

4 cups (1 L) prepared chicken broth
1 lb (454 g) potatoes, peeled and cut into 1-inch chunks
2 garlic cloves, chopped
1/4 cup (60 mL) sour cream
1 Tbsp (15 mL) extra-virgin olive oil
3/4 tsp (4 mL) salt
1/4 tsp (1 mL) pepper

In large pot over high, combine broth, potatoes and garlic. Bring to a boil, then reduce heat to low and simmer, covered, for about 15 minutes, until potatoes are tender. Drain, reserving broth. Transfer potatoes and garlic to large bowl.

Add sour cream, oil, salt, pepper and 1/2 cup (125 mL) reserved broth (if needed). Mash until smooth. Serve immediately.

Skewered Vegetables on the Grill

Serves 4

1 large onion
1 green pepper
1 red pepper
8 fresh white mushrooms
8 cherry or grape tomatoes
1/2 cup (125 mL) olive oil
1 garlic clove, minced
salt and pepper

Cut onion, green pepper, red pepper, mushrooms and tomatoes into similar-sized pieces. In large bowl, combine oil, garlic and salt and pepper to taste. Toss vegetables in oil mixture and place in cooler or refrigerator for 3 hours.

Preheat grill to medium. Soak wooden skewers in water for 30 minutes (or use metal skewers). Thread vegetables onto skewers. Cook for 10 to 15 minutes, rotating regularly, until vegetables have reached desired tenderness.

Pictured on page 87.

Easy Vegetable Rice

Serves 4

1 cup (250 mL) long-grain rice
2 1/4 cups (550 mL) water
2 Tbsp (30 mL) onion or vegetable soup mix
1/4 tsp (1 mL) salt
2 cups (500 mL) frozen corn, peas or mixed vegetables

In saucepan, combine rice, water, soup mix and salt and bring to a boil. Add vegetables and return to a boil. Reduce heat; cover and simmer for about 15 minutes, until rice and vegetables are tender.

Pictured on page 141.

Vegetable Risotto

Serves 8

2 Tbsp (30 mL) extra-virgin olive oil
1 cup (250 mL) diced onion
1 Tbsp (15 mL) minced garlic
1/2 cup (125 mL) diced celery
1/2 cup (125 mL) diced carrot
5 cups (1.25 mL) short-grain rice
6 cups (1.5 L) prepared chicken broth

1 tsp (5 mL) butter, softened
1 cup (250 mL) sliced fresh mushrooms
1/2 cup (125 mL) diced red pepper
1/2 tsp (2 mL) salt
1/2 tsp (2 mL) pepper

Heat oil in skillet over medium, and sauté onions until golden brown. Add garlic, celery and carrot, and cook for another 3 minutes, stirring constantly. Add rice and stir to coat with oil. Slowly add 1/2 cup (125 mL) chicken broth and stir until absorbed by rice. Continue adding 1/2 cup (125 mL) broth at a time until all broth is used and rice is cooked.

In another pan, melt butter and add mushrooms and red pepper; cook for 2 to 3 minutes. Season with salt and pepper. Add to risotto, stir and serve.

Sides

Cranberry Sauce

Serves 4

1/2 orange
1/2 lemon
2 Tbsp (30 mL) jellied cranberry sauce
1 tsp (5 mL) grated ginger root
1 tsp (5 mL) dry mustard
3 Tbsp (45 mL) dry red wine

Grate zest off orange and lemon. Squeeze juice of both fruits into bowl. In saucepan over medium, combine cranberry sauce, ginger and mustard. Add juice and zests, and continue to heat, bringing to a simmering point, whisking well to combine. Once sauce starts to simmer, turn heat off, stir in wine and serve. This sauce is great on venison or any other wild red meat.

Maple Bourbon Sauce

Serves 4

3 Tbsp (45 mL) pan drippings from cooking meat
2 Tbsp (30 mL) flour
1/4 cup (60 mL) Kentucky (Wild Turkey) bourbon
1/2 cup (125 mL) water
1/4 cup (60 mL) maple syrup
1 tsp (5 mL) hot pepper sauce

2 Tbsp (30 mL) heavy cream
salt, sprinkle

In small saucepan over medium, combine drippings and flour and stir until paste forms, then add bourbon and continue stirring. Sauce will begin to thicken. Increase heat and add water slowly, stirring constantly. Once sauce has reached a boil, stir in maple syrup and hot pepper sauce. Turn heat to low and simmer for 2 minutes.

Remove from heat and add cream. Stir well, return to heat for 1 to 2 minutes, add salt to taste and serve. This sauce is great with wild turkey, pheasant or goose.

Hot Mustard Sauce

Makes 2 cups (500 mL)

1 cup (250 mL) red plum jam
1 cup (250 mL) tomato chutney
6 Tbsp (90 mL) dry mustard
1/4 cup (60 mL) dry white wine

In small bowl, mix together jam and chutney. In another bowl, combine dry mustard and wine and stir until smooth. Add chutney mixture to mustard mixture and blend thoroughly. This sauce is great for waterfowl and upland game birds.

Honey Mustard Sauce

Makes 1 cup (250 mL)

1/2 cup (125 mL) honey
1/2 cup (125 mL) Dijon mustard

Combine ingredients in small bowl, and mix well. Makes a great dip for wild turkey strips or as a topping on moose or bison burgers.

Red Meat Marinade

Makes 2/3 cup (150 mL)

5 garlic cloves, minced
1/3 cup (75 mL) vegetable oil
2 Tbsp (30 mL) balsamic vinegar
2 Tbsp (30 mL) Worcestershire sauce
2 tsp (10 mL) Dijon mustard
1/2 tsp (2 mL) pepper

Combine all ingredients in bowl, and mix well. This marinade is great for venison or moose tenderloin, or any other red meat.

Greek Marinade

Makes about 3/4 cup (175 mL)

1/2 cup (125 mL) barbecue sauce
1/4 cup (60 mL) lemon juice
1 tsp (5 mL) dried oregano
1 tsp (5 mL) dried crushed rosemary
2 garlic cloves, minced

Mix all ingredients together. Place in large resealable plastic bag. Add your wild game, seal bag, shake to coat meat, and marinate in refrigerator for minimum 12 hours. This marinade is great with any red game meat.

Onion Gravy

Makes 3 cups (750 mL)

2 Tbsp (30 mL) vegetable oil
2 Tbsp (30 mL) butter
2 medium onions, diced
1 tsp (5 mL) sugar
1 tsp (5 mL) balsamic vinegar
3 cups (750 mL) prepared beef broth

4 tsp (20 mL) cornstarch
4 tsp (20 mL) cold water
1/2 tsp (2 mL) salt
1/2 tsp (2 mL) pepper

Heat oil and butter in large pan over medium. Add onion and cook, covered, for about 10 minutes, until onions are soft and translucent. Add sugar and balsamic vinegar and stir well. Cover and continue to cook for another 5 minutes. Add broth, cover and continue to cook for another 5 minutes.

In small bowl, combine cornstarch with water and mix to form thin paste. Pour 2 to 3 Tbsp (30 to 45 mL) hot gravy into starch mixture and mix thoroughly. Pour starch mixture into gravy, raise heat to high and boil for 10 minutes, until gravy is slightly thickened. Season with salt and pepper. Serve over your choice of wild game meat.

Horseradish Sauce with a Bite

Makes 2 cups (500 mL)

1 x 8 oz (225 g) block cream cheese, softened
1/4 cup (60 mL) prepared horseradish
1 Tbsp (15 mL) sugar
1 Tbsp (15 mL) lemon juice
1 tsp (5 mL) Worcestershire sauce
1/2 cup (125 mL) whipping cream

In medium bowl, blend cream cheese, horseradish, sugar, lemon juice and Worcestershire sauce. Fold in whipping cream. Refrigerate sauce until ready to serve with your choice of wild game.

Homemade Italian Dressing

Makes 2 3/4 cups (675 mL)

2 Tbsp (30 mL) dried oregano
2 Tbsp (30 mL) salt
1 Tbsp (15 mL) dried parsley
1 Tbsp (15 mL) onion powder
1 tsp (5 mL) dried basil
1 tsp (5 mL) pepper
1/4 tsp (1 mL) dried thyme
1/4 tsp (1 mL) celery salt

3/4 cup (175 mL) white vinegar
2 cups (500 mL) olive oil

Combine dry ingredients in small resealable plastic bag or small container with lid. Seal or cover, and shake to mix.

To make dressing, combine dry mixture with vinegar and olive oil in shakeable container. Store in refrigerator.

Easy Hamburger Relish

Makes 2 cups (500 mL)

1 1/2 cups (375 mL) chili sauce
1/2 cup (125 mL) prepared sweet pickle relish
1 tsp (5 mL) cinnamon
1 pinch salt
1 pinch pepper
1 pinch cayenne pepper

Combine all ingredients and mix well. Serve with your favourite hamburgers; refrigerate remaining relish in covered jar. It will keep in the refrigerator for up to 2 weeks.

Pictured on page 160.

Quick 'n' Easy Salsa

Makes 2 1/2 cups (625 mL)

1 x 28 oz (796 mL) can diced tomatoes
1 x 4 oz (113 g) can diced green chilis
1/4 cup (60 mL) thinly sliced green onion
1/4 cup (60 mL) chopped fresh parsley
2 Tbsp (30 mL) lemon or lime juice
1 garlic clove, minced
1/4 tsp (1 mL) salt
1/4 tsp (1 mL) pepper

Drain tomatoes, reserving 1/4 cup (60 mL) juice. In large bowl, combine tomatoes and juice with remaining ingredients; cover and chill for at least 4 hours. Serve with tortilla chips.

Canadian Fruit Salad

Serves 6

2 Cortland apples, peeled, cored and cut into
   1-inch (2.5 cm) cubes
2 McIntosh apples, peeled, cored and cut into
   1-inch (2.5 cm) cubes
2 Bartlett pears, peeled, cored and cut into
   1-inch (2.5 cm) cubes
1 banana, cut into 1/2-inch (12 mm) thick slices
1/2 lb (225 g) white grapes, cut in half

1 cup (250 mL) vanilla yogurt
1 Tbsp (15 mL) apple cider
1 tsp (5 mL) cinnamon
1/2 tsp (2 mL) ground nutmeg
1/4 tsp (1 mL) ground ginger
1/2 cup (125 mL) slivered almond slivers, toasted

In large bowl, combine apples, pears, banana and grapes.

In small bowl, mix together yogurt, apple cider and spices. Pour over fruit, and sprinkle with almonds.

Autumn Harvest Pumpkin Parfait

Serves 4

1 cup (250 mL) pumpkin puree
1 x 3.4 oz (96 g) package instant vanilla pudding powder
1 tsp (5 mL) pumpkin pie spice
1 cup (250 mL) evaporated milk
1 cup (250 mL) milk

Combine all ingredients in mixing bowl. Blend until smooth. Divide into 4 parfait glasses. Chill in refrigerator for 2 hours before serving.

Recipe Index

172

174

Index

About the Author

Growing up in a family-owned hotel in the Laurentian Mountains of rural Québec, Jeff was introduced to the outdoors and great cooking at a very young age, falling in love with both instantly. Over the years, he has made the great outdoors a focal point for his life's work. Jeff has a degree in environmental management as well as fish and wildlife biology. He is an award-winning member of the Outdoor Writers of Canada and has contributed to several Canadian and American publications over the years. He currently writes for Newfoundland's popular *Outdoor Sportsman* magazine and *Outdoor Canada* magazine, and has a regular column in *Bounder Magazine*. His first book, *Weird Facts about Fishing*, was released in 2010, and he writes a popular blog, *The Outdoors Guy*, for the *Ottawa Sun*.

Jeff has travelled to each and every province from coast to coast—hunting, fishing, camping and enjoying the fruits of his labour. He describes himself as the consummate conservationist and family-man, and describes his cooking as down to earth, simple, and about as Canadian as you can get. Jeff spent a lot of time at his uncle's famous steakhouse in the mountains of Québec, and picked up copious down-home tips along the way. He brings with him an in-depth knowledge of nature and conservation and a genuine love and passion for the outdoors—from the field to the table.

Acknowledgements
I would like to thank the editorial, production and test kitchen staff at Company's Coming for their part in making this cookbook spring to life. I would also like to thank the copious wildlife biologists, natural resources staff and conservation groups across Canada who keep close tabs on our precious wild game and who continue to defend Canada's hunting heritage. This book would not have been possible if not for the support of my amazing wife, Cheryl, and my beautiful daughters, Emily and Grace.